Librarian's Guide to WWW

Suresh Panwar
T.A.V. Murthy

Ess Ess Publications

4837/24, Ansari Road, Darya Ganj,
New Delhi-110002
✆ : 3260807, 3201533
Fax : 3274173
E-mail: essess@del3.vsnl.net.in

LIBRARIAN'S GUIDE TO WWW

First Published 2004

ISBN: 81-7000-387-3

Rs.495/-

Published by:
Ess Ess Publications
4837/24, Ansari Road,
Darya Ganj,
New Delhi-110 002.
Phone: 23260807, 55390185
Fax: 23274173
E-mail: essess@del3.vsnl.net.in

Printed in India at:
Printline, New Delhi-2.

Preface

This book *Librarian's Guide to WWW* is designed to be used by students with varied backgrounds, teachers, working professionals and can be used as a reference source. Whether you are a novice or have been using the Internet for years, you will find plenty of thoughts, great techniques, and useful information. And in addition to all this, you will find the chapters invariably interesting and refreshing. A wide variety of topics were selected to illustrate how the Internet and IT can be used, and organized flexibly in a systematic manner and in a simple way. Library Professionals may find themselves suitable readers as some of the chapters relate to them.

Fresh Graduates, entering the workplace will be expected to be able to use new technologies such as computers, the Internet and its World Wide Web. This book can be used for a good source for understanding & creating some Internet application.

The input for writing this book has come largely from the hands-on-experience of the authors with the Internet over the years, and teaching and interaction with Computer students, Librarians, Information managers, Professionals, Information Scientists and Technocrats working in different Universities. The thought behind writing this book into a very straightforward and simple language was that the experience and skills that have been accumulated by the authors should be carried to a common person. The book sometimes needs you to visit sites, while you are still learning about 'How to access web sites and search for information'. This book is an intended attempt to deliver essential technical know-how regarding Internet and it's various uses, into much much simpler language. This book will be very useful to the students as well as teachers as an Internet usage guide.

This book is carefully divided into two parts; first part is concerned with application of Internet while second part consists of advance applications. The book contains 7 chapters. Almost every chapter has a list of useful URLs at the end.

> *Chapter 1 tells about the basic need and objectives for writing this book.*
>
> *Chapter 2 provides a bird's eye-view to Internet and World Wide Web, and compares both. In addition to discussing briefly various other protocols and applications, it also presents an introduction on how Internet Applications are useful to Libraries and Information Centres.*
>
> *Chapter 3 highlights all types of resources available on WWW and imparts necessary skills in order to enable readers to compare different types of resources. Chapter dwells on imparting the know-how to search for specific information and formulate effective queries for searching*
>
> *Chapter 4 trains readers to navigate through various Search-engines, Meta search engines, databases, portals etc.*
>
> *Chapter 5 discusses on setting up a web server with a step-by-step approach with 'Screen Shots'. It discusses the installation procedure and*

configuration of web server software "IIS" from Microsoft as well as "Apache" Software from Apache Inc.

Chapter 6 provides a collection of necessary information and guidelines to design 'Library Web page' in a meaningful way.

Chapter 7 follows a step-by-step illustrative way to "Build your own Digital Library" using Greenstone Software. This is tailored specifically for working librarians, future librarians and for, anyone at the portals of digital craze.

The bibliographic references both print and online referred, are provided at the end.

Acknowledgements

This book is a result of rich experience of authors in computer and library domains, and interaction with fellow professionals, and is built upon a pile of ideas that have been accumulated over the years working with IT. The need for such a book was felt at various points of time during teaching others. Ideas have also come from various websites, books, friends, colleagues, and sharing their knowledge, expertise and skills.

Nobody is perfect. Maybe you felt that some important information is missing. Most probably, you have some ideas about betterment of contents. If readers find errors and /or omissions, they are humbly requested to bear with the authors as *To err is human*. So you are welcome to write to us with your comments if you wish to, so that corrections can be made in future.

We are thankful to Shri Alpesh Gajjar for his sincere assistance. Special thanks goes to Shri Sumit Sethi for his valuable suggestions.

Finally, we wish to place on record our sincere thanks to our families and friends for their constant support, guidance and good wishes.

Happy reading!!!

Suresh Panwar
TAV Murthy

Table of Contents

CHAPTER 1

Introduction

"Honesty is the first chapter of the book of wisdom."
-- Thomas Jefferson

Some people were Avatars, while others were great. The long list includes Buddha, Mahaveer, Jambhoji, Meera Bai and even Mother Teresa. Great People studied human behavior and announced solutions. While others, (comparatively less great people), followed a different path with mind-blowing thoughts and discovered science (technology) to solve basic human needs (such as Food, Shelter etc) and other nifty methods to live on the planet.

With the course of time, many things and methods were invented. Microcomputer (also known as PC) is comparatively a new development in Science & Technology. The remarkable and rapid development of computer technology (later turned into Information Technology) is a milestone in the progress history of human beings. Contribution of western countries in this regard is much.

Our emotions and decision making process has not changed since we first sensed the difference from other animals, & learnt about our communication abilities, but probably that was not enough. Communication technology with the invention of telephones, mobile handsets, wireless communication, started a race with transportation.

Computer systems helped communication technology after a decade or so, and also gone a bit lengthy by diving into the orbits of decision-making.

Networking of computer systems has made communication very fast and decision-making automated. Redundant information, extra employees, paper-shuffling, letters are all outdated. You may now forget about emotions, verbal communication & traditional decision-making on some definite cost.

In future, when users will be walking around with their computers in their pockets, it will be a completely new situation worthy enough to see and enjoy. Whatever the size and shape of the next wave of computers, those people who have unleashed the power of computer networks will be ready to serve the community and society.

Try to gauge the speed; what will be the speed of information, can you answer?

Information stored in the network will be available most probably, at the speed of light; no matter where located in the universe information is. May be somewhere on another planet...options are many. Helen Keller has rightly said "*Keep your face to the sun and you will never see the shadows*".

Perhaps, you would have noticed that the way we learn has changed totally, the latest IT methods have resulted into easy access to electronic resources, and Internet is obviously one of them. Therefore, new ways to searching & referring resources should be known in prior to begin searching and researching on Internet. Internet has enabled us to think more logically and flexibly. One who is not acquainted with the newly developed IT jargons, feels left out, while admitting that he doesn't know much about WWW and networks. Undoubtedly, the Internet has intruded into most walks of our life (to the extent of disturbing our lives damaging our cultural values and the nitty-gritty of traditionally rich society). Even new-generation kids are talking loudly about online games and chatting.

Large domain of problems exists as all sorts of frightening things happen on the screen (including fraud, porno etc etc...). Naturally, these comes in the domain of your duties to make aware the internet-users of your institution and remove the fears from the minds of parents by educating them and applying appropriate filters to ensure that there is no misuse. Very interestingly at the same time, various sounds can be heard too, librarians and IT personnel are talking high about digital libraries, library web sites, and Internet and e-journal kind of things, given the fact that most of our libraries are in the automation process.

Today, everyone from teachers, students, engineers to scientists, use Internet. There are a series of questions- raised by the pervasiveness of the Internet and World Wide Web. What is Internet? What is its architecture? Searching an information, How to formulate? How to discuss, plan and implement a digital library? Where to find out and disseminate e-sources from a web server? How a library home page should be, and what is current research regarding existing digital library systems? And what is the future?

Information Specialists are presupposed to flow with the latest technologies and to make efficient use of IT in libraries and classrooms.

We have seen that while most of the librarians and researchers, are very enthusiastic to get the benefits, very few are unaware of basic techniques such as 'search using various search engines'. However librarians and information scientists who are proud to set up a web site of their own and enrich it with their digital library, can see lights in the saying of John Ruskin "*The highest reward for a person's toil is not what they get for it, but what they become by it*."

This book is focused on the basic concepts of the Internet, searching & researching on internet as well as on advanced topics such as setting up of web server in your library, digital library, and guidelines to developing library home page.

Need

There are lots of questions in the minds about Internet, its architecture, World Wide Web, uses of Internet and web, different searches through portals and common know-how problems. All enthusiastic users now demand for content management, document management, digital collections, online-information dissemination etc. In addition, a person may be interested into building a web site and in future a digital library may be the goal of a LIS professional.

As there are a lot of discussions going on content management, content creation; on-line experiences are needed. How to design a home page for a library is also an urgent need. In fact, as of today, many of our universities don't have a proper up-to-date web site with on-line results (databases). All these factors pushed us to write a book based on our personal experiences in web over the years, and share our first-hand experiences with you.

Jean Paul says, "*As the more sand that escapes the hourglass of life, the vision becomes more clearer*". Similarly after gliding though the carefully designed flow of chapters, you will attain more sharpness in your attitude. These chapters will enable you to grasp the secrets and tricks of the gurus and march ahead on information highway.

This book follows a straightforward and simple approach to exploit the potential of computer networks, WWW and Library techniques & is written for the middle level executive, who works on Internet-based applications.

We present the concentrated technical information required for surfers to develop skills in WWW & Internet-based applications. The book presents specific information, steps, and strategies, and tricks in a very simple language from the layman-perspective; something not often found in other books on similar interests. In order to provide the readers a jumpstart on advanced applications of IT, the book asks to visit many useful URLs.

Every reader should capitalise on author's experiences. If you are an IT professional working in library sector, then navigate carefully through the chapters and you'll find them interesting. We have done enough to make this book best of breed. It's a "must-read" for professionals. This book focuses on the WWW, so that readers can independently research the Web. This book also offers a step-by-step approach to establish an Internet Information System using two popular web servers, and set up a Digital Library System to extend Library Web Site.

It will also provide Information personnel and researchers with a wealth of ideas related to their roles, as well as operations and support people who need to also understand the role they have in web system.

Objectives of the Book

- To expose professionals to the concept of the IT.
- To teach the basics of Networks.
- To teach the architecture of Network and it's various types.
- Application of Internet in libraries.
- To provide exposure to the uses of Internet and the Web.
- To enable formulating better search expressions.
- To acquaint professionals with the knowledge to carry out some specific tasks such as: -
    - How to search specific information from various search engines;
    - How to search for resources on WWW;
    - Compare different e-resources with each other;
    - How to cite electronic resources;
    - How to plan for library web page;
    - How to build a digital library;
    - To provide necessary know-how & skills for setting up apache and IIS web servers.

CHAPTER 2

The Internet

"Wisdom is knowing what to do next, skill is knowing how to do it, and virtue is doing it."
-- David Starr Jordan

This chapter will help you to get familiar with concepts of the Internet, web and the other services offered by the computer networks. After completion of this chapter, you will be able to understand the evolution of Internet and World Wide Web, know different architectures of network, the Internet, Intranet, Extranet, LAN, CAN, MAN, WAN, VPN, enumerate different Internet Applications, know the ways to Access the Internet, and get familiar with different protocols, browsers & terms being used.

If you are facing less familiarity with some words or concepts used here and there, you are requested to turn some of the pages, find your word under the heading of *"Key terms"* and return back. Advance readers, already having much experience may skip this chapter, if they do not find useful matter here.

Evolution of Internet

The Internet evolved from ARPANET, (the experimental network of U.S. Department of Defense's). In 1957, the USSR launched Sputnik, the first artificial earth satellite. Summarily speaking, in response to this, USA formed the ARPA to apply science and technology to the military. In 1962, RAND Corporation (a government agency) was commissioned by the US Air Force to do a study on how it could maintain its command and control over weapons, after a big attack (possibly nuclear). Needless to say, this was a fear of USA: during times of cold war. The outcome was a suggestion for packet switched military research network. Over the years, this network fragmented, and Internet formed by connecting various computers.

In short, the sequence of the events followed as: the invention
of Silicon Chip, invention of Packet switching, invention of Hypertext followed by TCP specifications.

In 1986, the United States National Science Foundation set up NSFNET, which linked 5 US University computer centers, a major milestone in the development of Internet. NSFNET Became very popular, and many people added their network into NSFNET and started calling it as Inter-Network.

In 1990, Tim Berners-Lee invented the World Wide Web, thereafter the Internet Society was chartered and World-Wide Web released by CERN. In 1993, WWW was establishing. In just 2 years, from 1993 to 1995, the use of HTTP Protocol increased dramatically, reduced the use of FTP & Telnet. Later around 1995, Internet Connectivity opened for Indian Public by the Govt. of India.

Internet as an Information resource

We know that today single computer can store terabytes of data today, when it is connected with other computer, it can store much and more. Hence, the Internet that consists of millions of computers connected with each other has emerged as a single largest source of information. In fact, Internet is a network of networks, linking computers using the protocol TCP/IP, allowing us to share the information, which is stored in some other computer machine located elsewhere remotely.

Every Website is a part of Internet. Every PC, cell phone, PDA or any other device that people use to look at web sites, is also a part of the Internet. We can think of Internet as a vehicle. And by using it, we can reach the place of information. We listen to so many people saying everyday that "I found that document on the internet", in fact saying like this is funny and also technically wrong, it can be said as "it was found though the Internet." Internet services, includes Web, FTP, Mail, Telnet, SNMP and many others.

Advances in computers and the emergence of the Internet are revolutionising the way we communicate and live. Vinton G. Cerf, the co-developer of computer networking protocol TCP/IP says on MCI Website "Though growing beyond my wildest expectations (over 605 million users worldwide as of September 2002), the Internet is still in its infancy. We can see an important development in the form of Voice over IP (VOIP) that is showing up both in private IP networks and on the public Internet. This development will have profound consequences for the traditional telephony industry. For one thing, VOIP is simply part of a richer fabric of Internet-enabled communication, not an end in itself. Moreover, it dictates a very different pricing structure for such services, considering that Internet services are basically flat price services that vary only with the capacity of the access circuit. ... Internet services and applications will play a major role in that re-invention."

The Internet includes academic and research networks such as: JANET (UK), SUNET (Sweden), DFN (Germany), NICNET, ERNET (India), commercial networks, government networks.

Importance of Internet in Library and Catalogue is much more. Mary L. Kao clears this fact in her book Cataloging and Classification for Library Technicians as *"The Internet will be the union catalogue of the world. More libraries will use the Internet as a source for copy cataloging*." Therefore, studying the Internet is completely worth it.

TCP/IP

TCP/IP stands for *Transmission Control Protocol/Internet Protocol*. TCP/IP is a common language of all the computers on the Internet, using that computers can communicate with each other.

Technically speaking, TCP/IP is the heart of Internet- it is a suite of protocols which are used to connect computers (and was originally designed for Unix Operating System). Your computer must be having TCP/IP (to be on Internet). TCP/IP names are resolved by DNS, while WINS Service of Windows will resolve Netbios names. The emphasis is nowadays on multiprotocol networking and in particular, integration of OSI standards into the present architecture.

Internet Vs. Web

Many people may think that Internet is a collection of websites, but it is not perfect. Internet is simply much more than WWW. However, it is true that due to popularity of WWW, the web has outpaced many protocols and applications such as Gopher. Gopher, Telnet and WAIS services of Internet are totally obsolete today, due to widespread usage of WWW.

In fact, Internet is a network of networks, and a network (computer network), in turn is a collection of computers.

A computer network provides an infrastructure for the use of E-mail, bulletin boards, file archives, hypertext documents, databases and many other computational resources and services. Internet uses TCP/IP protocols and packet switching and runs on any communications backbone. Internet has functioned as collaboration among cooperating parties. No one owns the whole of the Internet; no single agency determines how it operates from day to day. In India, VSNL, and NCST and some other agencies have played a role from the beginning of Internet in India in the field of IP allocation and Domain name registration.

ERNET and NICNET have been other important networks. Now days, there are many ISPs who can provide your organisation (say library) the pool of IP, and can also help registering domain name.

Internet Usage in Information Centres & Libraries

- The growth of Internet and proliferation of technology has widened the scope of correspondence. You might be aware that an ordinary hand-written letter (snail mail) takes a long journey thought buses, trains etc., and despite the hard work done by postal department gets delivered within 3 to 4 days.
- But with the advent of new means, IT, especially e-mails the situation have become

changed. Now even official communications are done using emails, and delay in communication has reduced, if not almost removed.

- Another aspect is of less dependency on the telephone. Many business concerns used the E-mail (and computer networks) to communicate and correspond (VSATS) to get through at the time of last strike by the employees of Telephone Department.
- The user-librarian interaction is changing. The librarians are at the doorstep of IT; they can transfer the data among researchers and faculties using latest communication method of e-mail. Librarians can join some e-group. The library can have its own portal or web site, and can provide WebOpac or Catalogues online. As a result, a Librarian can boast of his library facilities and project himself as an Information Manager.
- An Information Scientist can develop some system for online library and may also reach up to implementation of Digital Library (by using Greenstone or ePrint or Dspace).
- The Leadership opportunity can be utilised, and time and money can be saved, if you provide catalogue-searching functionality through your web site, then it will save time of user and time of staff. Users will be able to save their time of traveling to the library & staff will be able to search more efficiently using computers. The impact is high.

- Libraries often take lead in providing various services such as query answering, information sharing and dissemination, inter-library loan etc. In western countries, the libraries are even targeted by legislators for free liberal access of Internet to users, and it is not possible to track a user, who has committed a crime using general Internet access from public computer. The service, however, is more important and should be provided in all cases.
- By providing online access to leading publications and other e-resources, a librarian can satisfy the user's demand for newer resources. Many publishing houses do the great stuff of providing electronic equivalent information of print journals or books. This will pacify the readers, who are vying for latest updates and publications.
- Web-Opac from Library of Congress, IPL, OCLC and other bibliographic information will be of utmost importance to information-seeking people. Different Libraries provide access to their catalogues online, and this may be useful for inter-library-loan or sharing purposes.
- Now days, most of the publishers announce their publication-details, reviews etc. online on their web site, Amazon (amazon.com) is just an example. A library can take the printouts of these details and provide services. It is worthwhile to point out here

that in future, on-line transactions (such as buying books) will be legal.

- In addition to all this, much Government information can be downloaded from various govt agencies web sites, and their contact details, terms, policies can be known & circulated.
- E-mails of important personalities can be obtained, and a knowledge base can be developed or printed at notice board. This will be ultimately getting praised from the users (who act as patrons).

Basic network Architecture: Internet, Intranet and Extranet

Some people like to prefer to know the network boundaries. Thinking in this way, a network can be divided into three types: Internet, Intranet and Extranet as shown in Fig. 2.1.

Internet

Internet is a public face of an organisation. The information available on the Internet is meant to be in public domain & to be used by anyone without any authentication. And many of the websites provide their company's information and this method has proved its worth. It is a quick and efficient way for company's clients to know about a company, its products, operations and field.

Internet is outside the limit of a Firewall. A Web Server is sometime placed outside the firewall.

Some computers on the Internet provide some services or documents and thus are called Servers, while other computers are called clients; client computer are on the receiving-end, they depend upon the server machines to fulfill their requests. The requests may be anything; it may be for accessing a HTML Document or for Email Message transfer. Example of Client programs includes Browsers such as Internet Explorer, Email Clients such as Netscape, FTP Clients etc, whereas, example of Server programs includes Web Servers, Email Servers etc.

Intranet

Intranet is a privately owned network inside an organisation, which is behind a firewall or proxy server. The information placed on the intranet is meant to support day-to-day organisational work, and the same is not available to public users; that is only for internal use. An intranet may be on the Internet (or may simply be on a network). An organisation may have more than one intranet supporting more than one intranet portals. An Intranet portal is a web site which can have both structured and non-structured information and must fulfill the needs of the work. For an example: The "Campus Educational Portal" in a campus is meant for faculty and students in an educational campus. Roughly speaking, it can host any file, which is appreciated by students (users). The Servers, which can be run on Internet, can also be run on Intranet Sites (see Fig. 2.1).

Extranet

Extranet is somewhere lying between the above two. Sometime it takes the form of intranet by one angle; while looking from other angle, it is an Internet. In Extranet, some authenticated users can get access to secured area of web site; which is prohibited for the general public but accessible to intranet users such as employees. Authentication takes place in the form of User-Id/Password.

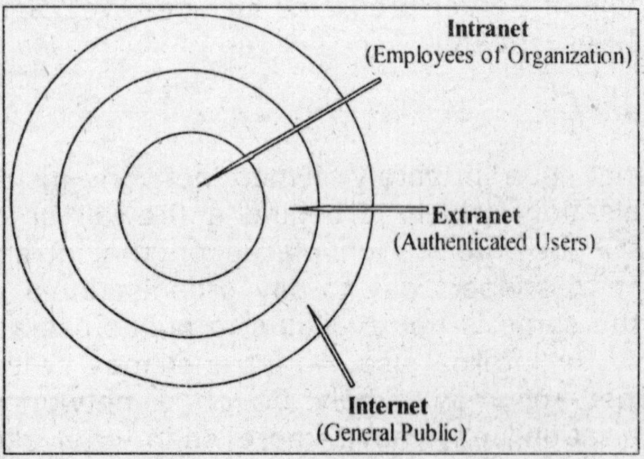

Fig 2.1 Internet, Intranet & Extranet

VPN

VPN stands for **Virtual Private Network**. As indicated by its name, it is a private network virtually; which makes virtual paths by using public data transport line.

In fact, instead of using a dedicated, real-world connection such as leased line (as employed by private networks), it uses a public network (usually the Internet) to connect remote sites or users together. A VPN enables a company's private network to connect to the remote employee or remote site.

Fig 2.2 Virtual Private Network

A Virtual private networks (VPN) provides an encrypted connection between a user's distributed sites over a public network (e.g., the Internet). The basic idea for IP based VPN is to provide an encrypted IP tunnel (for secure network applications) through the Internet (public transport of data) that . permits distributed sites to communicate securely as depicted in Fig 2.2. For Windows Users, Microsoft has squeezed the VPN features into Win 2000.

From logical standpoints, other categorisation also exists and can be defined based upon the geographical limits such as LAN, WAN etc., as described below.

LAN

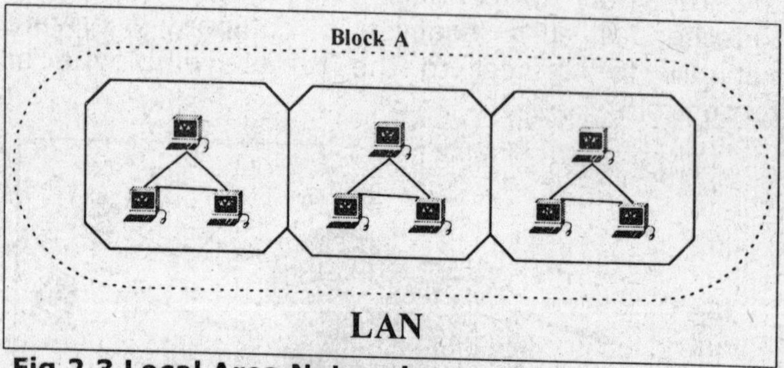

Fig 2.3 Local Area Network

A **<u>L</u>ocal <u>A</u>rea <u>N</u>etwork** (LAN) is usually spread in a single room, and it can connect the computers and other resources inside a lab that spans a short distance. A LAN can spread in various floors of a building of Library as shown in Fig 2.3.

Typically, LANs in most of the cases, will use "Ethernet protocol" to connect nodes. As Ethernet protocol is in wide use. Now a day, "Fast Ethernet" is getting more popularity. Hub is a popular device which is used to create a LAN. Switches are more efficient than hubs and they are used for more speed.

CAN

A **<u>C</u>ampus <u>A</u>rea <u>N</u>etwork** (CAN) can be defined as a Large LAN, or a Collection of interconnected Local Area Networks operating in a big campus such as a university campus or college campus (Fig 2.4). In this case, CAN will connect to various departments with Library and University Computer Centre. CAN may use Optical Fibre Cable(OFC) to connect various LANs in the Campus.

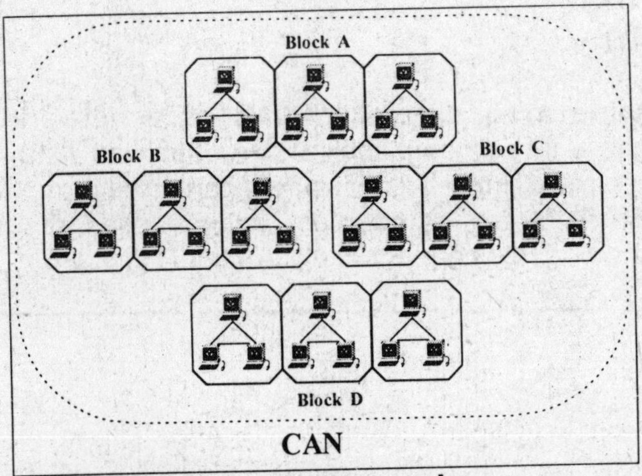

Fig 2.4 Campus Area Network

MAN

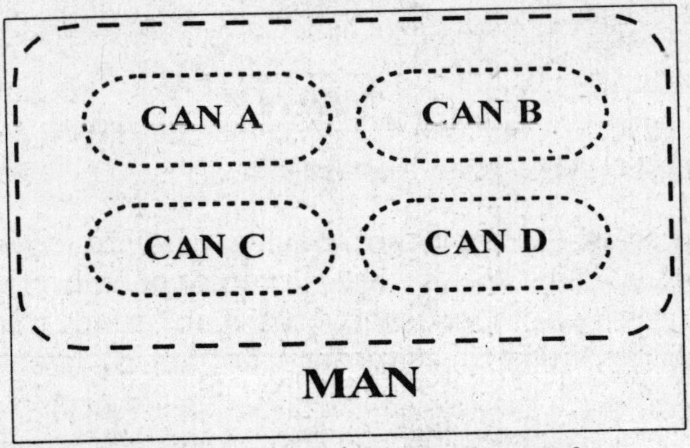

Fig 2.5 Metropolitan Area Network

Metropolitan Area Network (MAN) can be defined as a collection of interconnected CANs, operating over a city (Fig 2.5).

WAN

A **wide area network** (WAN) is a network that spans a large geographical area such as *Asia*. It is the largest kind of network interconnection. Many multi-national companies make use of WAN technology to connect their offices (Fig 2.6).

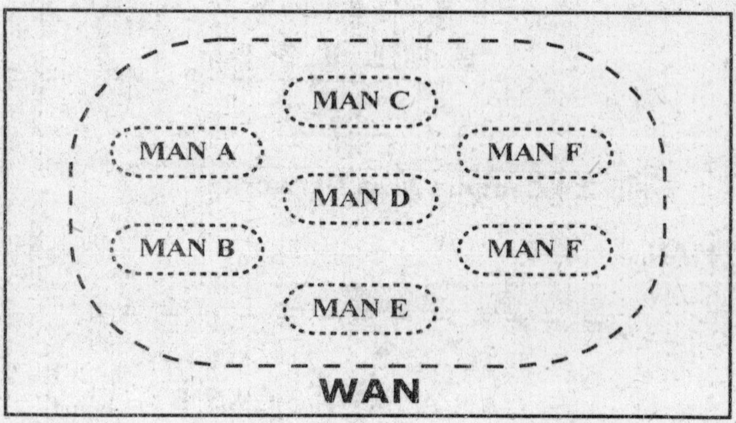

Fig 2.6 Wide Area Network

Router is an important device used to develop a WAN. Two WANs are interconnected through routers. The local networks can send data via satellite links to different continents, creating a WAN.

If your organisation happens to be a library, with the course of time, your library may provide a way to link to a database server providing access to catalogue cards. For an organisation entity, basic Intranet architecture to start with, we recommend the following as a minimum:

- POP3-based mail server
- A Proxy server or Firewall
- A web server
- A discussion forum

Accessing the Internet

To access the Internet by computer, you need a computer, a modem, telecommunication link, and software to connect to an ISP (Internet Service Provider). Virtually any computer can connect to the Internet; irrespective of the operating system it is running e.g. Linux, Macintosh, Windows...

Computers can use Internet connectivity, which is a service provided by an ISP. ISP is a short form for "Internet Service Provider". The Internet connectivity can be of one of several types written below-

1. Direct/dedicated connection (VSAT, Microwave, Leased Line)

2. Dial-up connection (Telephone Line)

In India, Large Companies, IUCs, Universities, colleges and research institutions typically have a direct / dedicated cable connection to the Internet, giving all users high-speed access at any time.

Users, who access the Internet from small offices or homes, use dial-up to connect to the Internet. Dedicated/ Direct connection offers higher bandwidth whereas dial-up connectivity is comparatively slow.

Dial-up

A Modem is always placed in-between a computer machine (digital) and an analog system (say telephone system) including analog copper wire.

Before placing data on telephone lines, a modem that sends the signals modulates the incoming digital signals (from the PC), changes the signals into analog form, thus allowing data to be transmitted and received over telephone lines (analog lines).

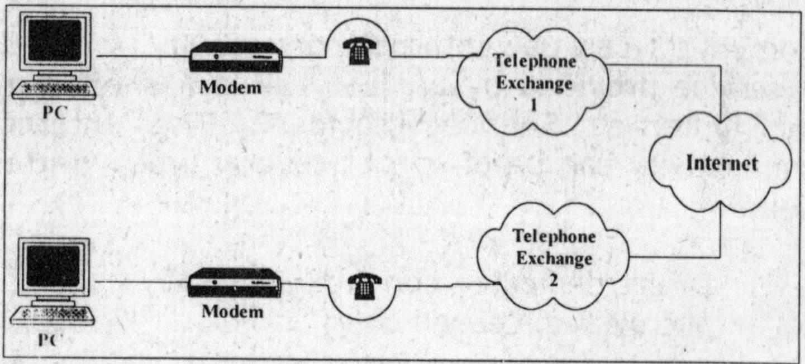

Fig 2.7 Two computers connected via Dial-up

This form of connection is generally slower than a direct connection, as the telephone system has a relatively limited capacity for data transmission.

The modem on the other hand (on receiving end) demodulates the incoming analog signal to digital form and passes it to the computer on the other side to be received (Fig 2.7).

In addition, other electronic devices such as mobile phone equipments and even some televisions can also be used to connect to the Internet. You might know that such TVs are known as "Web-TV".

Dedicated (Direct)

A dedicated connection is considered more reliable and fault-tolerant and provides an organisation with a full-time, (24 hours per day) connection to the Internet. It means that you are connected all the times.

This connection is best for an organisation entity e.g. a University, who needs to maintain online presence at all times.

This type of connectivity is needed by an Internet-based organisation, whose critical business operations and online transactions cannot tolerate delay and therefore, cannot survive without dedicated connectivity.

This type of connectivity is provided to corporate segments by ISPs with big infrastructure setup.

Generally Speaking, anyone of these three methods can be employed to achieve dedicated/ direct connectivity at the user-end:-

1. Using VSAT (satellite connectivity)
2. Using Microwave (Radio Link)
3. Using Leased Line (Fiber Optical or ISDN)

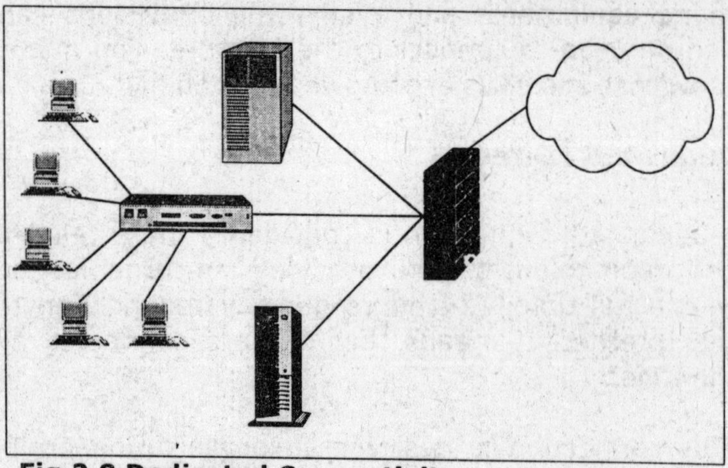

Fig 2.8 Dedicated Connectivity

Internet Servers of an organisation on a dedicated link is shown in Fig. 2.8. Also notice that employees are on the LAN PC protected by a Firewall.

Applications of Network

First of all, we will focus on the protocols and applications being used for Network applications and which are basic. Then we may discuss those in some greater detail. The table 2.1 shows bird-view of some of the protocols and respective applications.

The protocols have been accepted as a result of extensive research by the scientists and engineers on international level. Some of the 'applications-protocols relations' are shown below, in first two columns of the Table 2.1.

Application	Protocol	Client	Server
Electronic mail	*SMTP, POP3, IMAP4*	*E-mail Client*	*Mail Server Or Mail Host*
File Transfer	*FTP*	*FTP Client*	*FTP Server*
Terminal Emulation	*Telnet*	*Telnet Client*	*Telnet Host*
World Wide Web	*HTTP*	*Web Browser*	*Web Server*
Network News	*NNTP*	*News Reader Or Usenet Client*	*Usenet Host*
Chat	*IRC*	*Chat Client*	*Chat Server*

Table 2.1 Application-protocol relations

Electronic mail

Electronic mail is a quick and cheaper way to send information in digital form, from one computer to another computer (connected by some medium) and in short called as e-mail. It has been observed that, it is one of the most popular activities performed on Internet.

Ray Tomlinson had invented email in year 1971. The first email was sent between two computers, which were actually placed beside each other. The text "QWERTYUIOP or something similar, was simply a test message sent to himself for the first time. Despite this success with email, many people know Tomlinson for a different reason i.e. introducing the "@" sign in email addresses.

Electronic transmitting of messages between mailboxes (from one user's mailbox to, another user's mailbox) is known as emailing.

It is an asynchronous communication, while chat is an activity performed in synchronous mode. This enables internet-users to send messages to other email-users or groups of users quickly, conveniently and cheaply. Computers can also be configured to respond automatically to email messages. A similar facility is used for the management of mailing lists.

Structure of e-mail Address

Let us consider a simple email address as shown below, it has two parts separated by sign @; the first part indicate the user name or user-id on email server, the second part is host name /domain name.

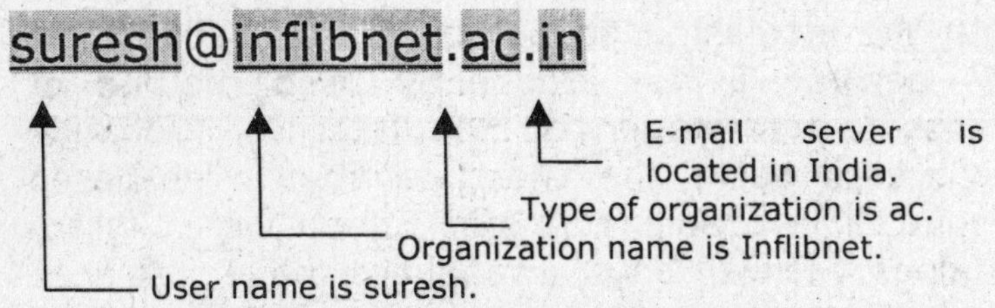

Possible Usage of email

- Communication
- Exchanging documents
- Entertainment
- Email Discussion forum
- Collaboration
- And many more...

Telnet (Remote login)

Originally developed for Unix environment, this is a type of Internet service allowing one computer to remotely log onto another computer (the first commonly known as terminals or dumb terminals, and other known as hosts).

In other words, telnet implies "remote login". Telnet is a program that allows you to log into computers on the Internet. There are no graphics in Telnet sessions, just text.

With the increasing popularity of the Web, Telnet has become a less frequently used method of access to information on the Internet. Probably, few years back, the most common Web-based resources available through Telnet were library catalogs. These days, webopacs have replaced them. The server machine is known as Telnet Host, and client program is known as Telnet Client, as described in Table 2.1.

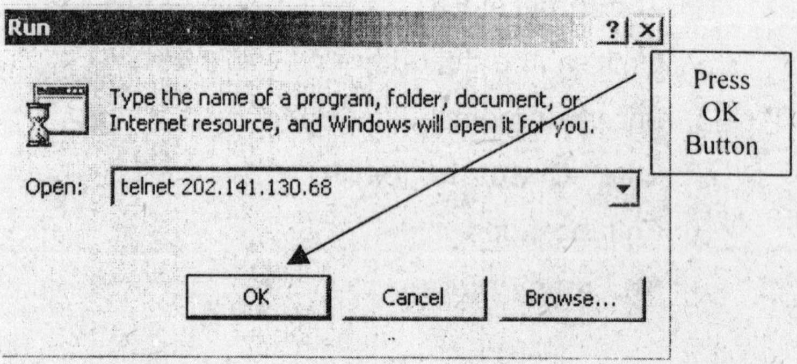

Fig 2.9

To Telnet to a computer, you must know its address. This can consist of words (*soul.inflibnet.ac.in*) or numbers reflecting IP address (202.141.130.68).

Suppose, we have to logon to a Linux machine. Given the fact that Telnet service is enabled (running) on the said machine and the machine is up on the Internet, then we can logon to the machine by issuing the commands.

We can give a command like:

Telnet soul.inflibnet.ac.in as shown in Fig. 2.9.

After that it will connect to the said machine and if you have a user name and account in that machine, you can logon remotely by using Telnet.

It turns a remote user as if he is a virtual terminal, and allows him to do work in his capacity to the server machine (host). One needs an account on the remote host- to be able to login to it, after the connection is mode.

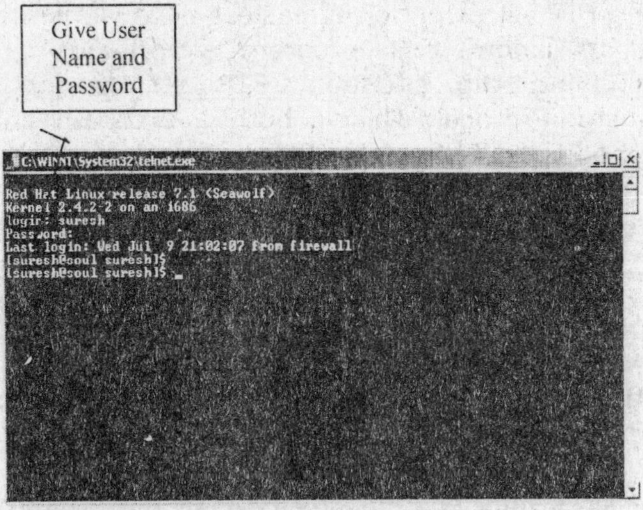

Fig 2.10 Telnet session

FTP (or File Transfer Protocol)

FTP was the first service developed for Inter-networks. A Computer running FTP Service is known as FTP Host (or FTP Server), and the client should have FTP Client installed on client machine to connect to FTP Host.

An Example of FTP Client is, CuteFTP, which has become popular (free utility to download from various download sites) due to provision of Graphical Interface, which help a window user and doesn't require for remembering the commands.

Earlier, FTP was used to fetch a file from a remote host to user's pc. It is still used, but now days, a browser is sufficient enough to get us download software from a Web site to our local machine, using FTP. This option is easiest because we need not to know FTP program commands, thus simplifying the situation. FTP stands for File Transfer Protocol. This is both a program and a method used to transfer files between computers. There are two types of FTP: Anonymous FTP and non-anonymous FTP.

Anonymous FTP is an option set by host-administrator, which allows users to transfer files from thousands of host computers on the Internet to their personal computer regardless of an account and password on the host machine.

FTP sites may contain any type of files (binary or text). The files may contain books, articles, software, games, images, sounds, multimedia, course work, data sets or any other thing.

Non-anonymous FTP is a FTP service, which ensures that a user can access FTP services running on a computer, only if user has valid user-id and password.

FTP protocol includes two systems: FTP client & FTP server. FTP client requests a file transfer & server approves the request and does the sending or receiving. While the client side of FTP is just an interface for end user the server side of FTP is a service enabled on server machine; it wakes up when a FTP client get attached with it. There are two important commands: get and put. A client can issue get command to receive some files from server and use put to place them in a specified directory on the FTP server. By 1999 Archie had been almost completely replaced by web-based search engines. Earlier Archie was used to find files stored on anonymous FTP sites.

World Wide Web

World Wide Web is one of the most popular Internet services. World Wide Web is a collection of web sites. WWW application is quite young in comparison to other applications of Internet, but has become the most popular application in a very short span of time.

It was released in 1992 at CERN Institute of Physics. WWW was borne out by the experiments of hyper-linking of various loosely related documents Hyper-linking was carried out by Tim Berners-Lee in 1989. He now directs the World Wide Web Consortium, an open forum of companies and organisations with the mission to lead the Web to its full potential.

One can retrieve documents, view images, animation, and video, listen to sound files, speak and hear voice, and view programs. A browser is needed to access a Website. Before the birth of HTTP Protocol and WWW, the main things one could do over the Internet were email (SMTP), telnet, ftp, and news groups/Usenet. As of now, you can insert a file, (which can be downloaded via FTP), into a web page. Now, a browser is capable enough to access a Web site.

World Wide Web depends upon the Protocol HTTP & HTML (A Subset of SGML). A Website is loaded on a web server and even may link to some other web site, thus create a web of sites. More details may be found in Chapters 5 & 6.

Usenet news

As described in Table 2.1, Usenet News depending upon NNTP Protocol, is simply a 'bulletin board system' very much similar to e-mail discussion group. Subscribing to a Newsgroup is a big move to be updated on a particular topic.

Suppose one wants to get updated on FrontPage operations as a client, then he may find Microsoft.public.frontpage.client as a suitable newsgroup for his updating of knowledge and even can get help from other experts by posting his specific problems when he might be facing for publishing his content pages on his website.

The major difference between Usenet News and e-mail discussion groups (Mailing List) is the fact that Usenet messages are stored on central computers, and users must connect to these computers to read or download the messages posted to these groups. This is distinct from e-mail distribution of mailing lists, in which messages arrive in the electronic mailboxes of each list member. Further, Newsgroups cannot be private (like some mailing lists).

When you post to a newsgroup server, that post is transferred to other newsgroup server as decided by the administrator of the news server. Usenet itself is a set of machines that exchanges messages, or articles, from Usenet discussion forums, called newsgroups.

There are thousands of Usenet newsgroups in existence; if you connect to news.Microsoft.com then you will find many news servers running within that.

For example: **Microsoft.public.access.security, Microsoft.public.word.setup. networking** etc.

You have to choose which news servers, you wish to subscribe, according to your interests. After the act of subscribing, you can download the information on various messages post into that specific newsgroup. Further you can catch-up a particular post, if you are interested into. The Usenet news can be read by a variety of newsreader software programs; for example, Microsoft Outlook Express or Netscape have the in-built newsreader programs.

E-mail discussion groups (Mailing List)

One of the benefits of the Internet is the opportunity it offers to people worldwide to communicate via e-mail. One of the most popular methods of holding topic-discussion over the Internet are email discussion groups. Software programs, administer these groups. Probably the most common program is the listserv. Typically, member of the group sends messages to the mailing-list address, which is then forwarded to all members of the list. If other subscribers wish to share their thoughts and views on the topic, they can just click on the Reply button and add their comments, which are again distributed to all the subscribers of mailing list through distribution of reply email to every user's mailbox.

A great variety of topics are covered by Mailing Lists, many of them academic in nature. When you subscribe to a Mailing List, messages from other members are automatically sent to your electronic mailbox. You subscribe to a mailing list by sending an e-mail message to a computer program called a listserver or Mailing List Manager, which are located on computer networks throughout the world. This manager program handles subscription information and distributes messages to and from subscribers. You must have an e-mail account to participate in a listserv discussion group.
Examples of Email Groups:-

WBTOLL-L

WBTOLL-L is an email discussion group, which discusses Web Based Training (WBT) and related issues. High quality discussions can be found out there.

LIS-Forum

This is another example of a mailing list, which is very popular among Indian library & information science professionals. This list is administrated by NCSI, located in IISC, Bangalore.

LAZYDBA

This is a very active mailing list among DBAs of Oracle, SQL Server and DB2 (DBA means to Data Base Administrators). After Every few minutes, there will be an email in your mailbox, if you are a member of this list.

An example is given below. LazyDBA.com is a website, where you can visit and get registered with the mailing lists by providing your email address to this website.

You don't need a web browser to visit a web site & to read mailing list. Just an e-mail client such as Outlook express or Incredimail is enough to retrieve your emails.

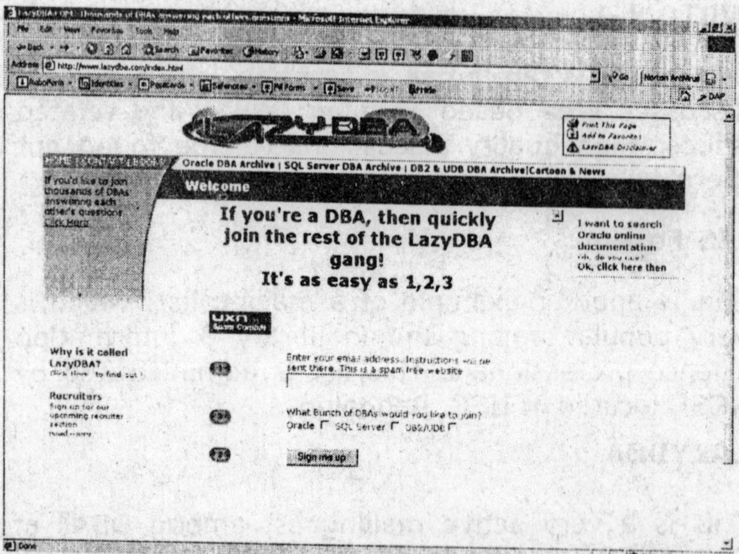

Fig 2.11

Mailing lists, unlike Usenet news groups, can be private. There is much etiquette to be followed while using Mailing List, and you have to follow these in practice.

Never become involved in a war of words; unfortunately if you have become involved, try not to escalate it and nurture the feeling of co-existence.

Different people have different views, for a given situation; try to stay calm and ask politely if you have a relevant question or if you wish to seek a clarification from someone.

Try to avoid heavy words such as "most", "many", "well-known", or "everyone knows".

An Example email of mailing-list

```
On Tue, 21 Oct 2003, Brian Zelli wrote:

> Date: Tue, 21 Oct 2003 07:49:01 -0400
> From: Brian Zelli <brian.zelli@adelphia.com>
> To: Jaroslav Smucr <smucrj@endata.cz>
> Cc: LazyDBA.com Discussion
<oracledba@lazydba.com>
> Subject: RE: patchset
> Jaroslav that was perfect except....., now the
vendor wants 8.1.7.2 instead.
> Do you know the patch number for that?
> Brian
>
Hi:
http://metalink.oracle.com/metalink
 [Patches]
   Select a Patch Search Area
     * Simple Search
       Search By  Patch Numbers(s)  1882450
         [Go]
 Patchset 1882450
 Description 8.1.7.2 PATCH SET FOR ORACLE DATA
SERVER
 Product Oracle Database Family
 Release Oracle 8.1.7.2
 Select a Platform or Language Microsoft Windows
(32-bit)
 Last Updated 12-SEP-2001
 Size 100M (105054413 bytes)
 [Download]
Patchsets known to include or supersede Patchset
1882450
No information available from the patch repository.

Regards,
```

```
js
--

--------
Get today's cartoon: http://www.LazyDBA.com
Please don't reply to RTFM questions
Oracle documentation is here:
http://tahiti.oracle.com
To unsubscribe: send a blank email to
oracledba-unsubscribe@LAZYDBA.com
To subscribe:   send a blank email to
oracledba-subscribe@LAZYDBA.com
By using this list you agree to these
terms:http://www.lazydba.com/legal.html
```

Some Key Terms

Domain name

Every Computer on the Internet has an Address, known as IP address; it is linked with a name known as URL. URL is a short form for Uniform Resource Locator. Website URL recognises a host computer on the Internet. Domain name is a part of URL. Domain name helps in locating the computer's place (in huge WWW).

For example: you wish to browse UPSC Web Site; it has a web site address of www.upsc.gov.in, so we say that host name is upsc.gov.in. Similarly take an example of Inflibnet web site, whose address is http://web.inflibnet.ac.in. Here "web" is a host computer name, the domain name is "inflibnet.ac.in". Here, inflibnet is a company's identifier, where ac is a top-level domain indicating for academic community; and in indicating country code for India..

All educational institutions in India can be a part of 'ac.in' or 'edu.in'. The other top-level domain follows similar nomenclature "com" for commercial sites and "org" for non-profit organisations. One has to pay to use a certain Domain Name.

Domain Name Server

One of the computers on ISP end, works to translate URL, names into their corresponding IP numbers. This special computer, (known as name server) keeps tables of other machine names and their associated unique IP addresses, and translates one into the other.

For example, imagine that we wish to visit www.goodnewsindia.com, so we type this into address bar of browser and press enter. Our browser will first contact DNS and get the IP number, if IP number exists for the address we have typed, the browser would be able to do its work, otherwise some error message will be displayed.

IP Address

IP stands for *Internet protocol.* Every computer connected to the Internet (or on Local Area Network) must have a unique address known as: *IP number.* IP number is a unique number consisting of 4 parts separated by dots; will look similar to the example: 202.141.130.69 or 192.168.1.62. Each IP address also has a corresponding domain name (address). Machines that are on the Internet have a unique IP address. If a machine does not have an IP number, it is not really on the Internet. Most machines also have one or more Domain Names that are easier for people to remember. When you type in your browser http://www.bhaskar.com then behind the curtain DNS changes the name bhaskar.com and convert to an IP number, and connect to that computer and open the web page.

Mail Server

A mail server is a computer machine on the network, which dedicatedly runs a software (such as Sendmail or MS-Exchange) for sending/receiving the emails. You can connect to this machine from any client machine to get/send emails through the server machine.

Browser

Without browsers, we cannot see a website. In other words, browsers are essentials for surfing. There are two types of browsers: GUI based and Text only & non-GUI. A browser is a computer program that resides on a computer, and this enables a user to view WWW documents and access the Internet, taking advantage of text formatting, hypertext links, images, sounds, motion, and other features.

Examples of some popular browsers are: Internet Explorer, Netscape, Mozilla, and Lynx. Internet Explorer is the most commonly used web browser followed by Mozilla & Netscape etc; all these are graphical interfaces (meaning they facilitate the viewing of graphics such as images and video and more). The Lynx browser is the most frequently used text-only browser and has been adapted to serve the needs of the vision-impaired.

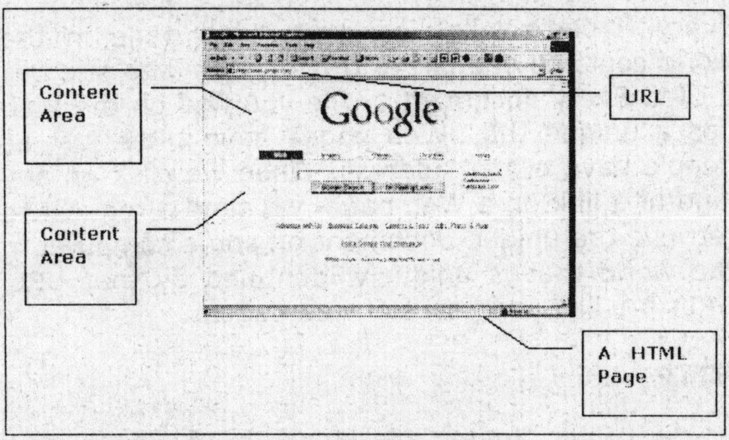

Fig 2.12 A Browser window

All graphical browsers require rely on "plug-ins" to handle the fancier files. Plug-ins are sub-programs required for browsers to support special types of files (such as Flash). Most plug-ins are free, easy and safe to install on your computer, and are freely available from the file proprietor's website to be downloaded.

Browsers differ in the features of convenience they offer for navigating and managing the Web. Almost all browsers provide more or less similar functionality & menu items.

URL

URL stands for Uniform Resource Locator. Examples of some URLs are www.upsc.gov.in, www.careerage.com, www.ugc.ac.in, www.oracle.com etc.

Every Hypertext link on every web page in the world contains one of the URLs. Every web site has a URL. Every document or file you find on the Web has a unique URL. Web pages have URLs just as people have e-mail address. When we click on any kind of a link on a Web page, we send a request to retrieve the unique document on some computer in the world that is uniquely identified by that URL. URLs are like addresses of web pages.

HTTP

World Wide Web depends mainly upon the Protocols HTTP. HTTP stands for *Hyper Text Transfer Protocol*. A website is loaded on a web server and is available on a network by HTTP Protocol. It connects on port 80 of the web server by default.

HTTP, HTML, thousands of web sites, and search engines made other protocols (e.g. gopher, finger) obsolete. Back in the early Internet days, other popular protocols used on the Internet were Telnet,

FTP, and NNTP (news groups/Usenet) & SMTP (email).

HTML

HTML stands for *Hyper Text Markup Language*. HTML is a standard defined by the World Wide Web Consortium (W3C), which is directed by Tim Berners-Lee, who had invented the idea of hyper-linking of documents (further turned into Web). It is a Subset of SGML. It is a set of tags. HTML is a descriptive language. In fact, HTML is driving the technology of markup languages today. Using a browser one can access World Wide Web. The heart of HTML is hypertext capability.

As shown in Fig. 6.1, all web servers send data (or signals) to connected browsers - in the ultimate format of HTML only. HTML pages can be created or edited by any text editor (e.g. notepad). You don't need Internet connectivity to browse a web page, which is on your computer machine. If a page is on another computer machine (on a web server), then you need a browser. A browser will be enough to test a page. A browser can access a Web site. A browser can be a GUI (such as Internet Explorer, Netscape) or non-GUI Text based browser (such as Lynx). Regardless of the type of browser one can access a HTML page.

You can create HTML files using an easy, user-friendly WYSIWYG editor from Microsoft known as FrontPage (whose latest version is FrontPage 2002). Tasks such as inserting tables, graphics, etc. can be performed very easily. Even people having very little knowledge of computing can easily develop HTM/HTML pages by using this Editor.

Common file types found on the web

Below is a list of some common file types found on the web with, their short descriptions.

File Extension	Description
.TXT	ASCII text file; basic text without any formatting like bold or italic.
.DOC,.PDF	Microsoft Word File (Formatted Document); Microsoft Presentation File
.GIF	Image file of 256 colors, often used for logos, and animations etc.
.JPG, .JPEG	Image file often used for full-color photographs. There is no difference between .jpg and .jpeg
.PDF, .PPT	Portable Document File for displaying facsimiles of documents used for exact display of govt. reports, publications etc.
. AVI, .MPEG	Movie Files
.HTM, .HTML	HTML files: the ultimate file format for WWW. There is no difference between .htm and .html

- **Text Files (.TXT, .DOC, .PDF)**

Text files may be in the form of .txt files or .doc files. TXT files are unformatted files, and have plain text, which can be printed. They are also called ASCII Files; ASCII stands for *American Standard code for Information Interchange.* Any simple text editor such as Notepad can create Txt files. Text files take least load and get displayed in short time on a browser.

Other types of **rich text files** are HTML, Word Files and PDF Files; these have the capability to add graphics with text and have formatting capabilities. Here HTML is a standard for web documents, and Word is used to refer to Microsoft Word having .DOC Extension and PDF is used to refer to Acrobat files having PDF extension. Adobe Company invented PDF format (to be printed on PostScript (tm) printers). To read these PDF files, you need Adobe Acrobat Reader, which is free software and can be downloaded from adobe web site (www.adobe.com). PDF is basically used to design brochures, forms, reports etc. with complex designs & to remove machine and platform dependence for the documents, and their goal is typographic control. Many word processors, can create PDF files easily, so many sites are now serving them online. To ensure that a word document looks the same on every platform/machine, you can convert it into PDF. By installing Acrobat on a computer machine one can easily convert a DOC file into PDF file, by single clicking only onto, a button which is added to toolbar of Ms-word.

- **Multimedia Files**
  - **GIF**

The files having GIF Extension are a sort of Image file; gif files are used for logos, animation and dynamic graphic images, and can show up to 256 colours only. GIF is a compressed file format. Most browsers don't find any problem in displaying them.

- **JPG**

JPG or JPEG are the extensions of files, which represent images. JPEG stands for Joint Photograph Expert Group. This is a file format; these files are used for full-colour photograph taken using a digital camera. JPG is a compressed file format. Most browsers don't find any problem in display them. JPEG standard was initially developed to compress still images,

- **MPEG**

Any browser can display still images like JPG/GIF. It's the sound and video that can present a problem. MPG or MPEG are the extensions of files, which represent a movie. MPEG stands for Moving Picture Expert Group. This is a file format; these files are used for movies. MPEG is a compressed file format. MPEG standard was developed to compress video rather than still images.

• **AVI**

This is a movie file format. This is an uncompressed file format.

• **PPT**

This is a popular file extension; it shows that the file is a presentation file, created by Microsoft PowerPoint.

• **SWF**

It is simply a Shockwave flash file, which is meant for graphical and motion effects and can be used for a small presentation. It can be run more efficiently on a browser compared to a PPT file on a web server. To take advantage of this benefit, many people prefer to convert PPT file into a flash file and then put it on a web server.

• **Script files**

Script files add interest to a simple HTM or HTML Page, by adding dynamic contents or by inserting contents at several places in a page. These script files have the capabilities to add data into an html page by fetching from the database or vice versa. CGI, PL, ASP are page extensions of scripts, these scripts also help a Website or Webmaster to get 'Form submission' from the visitors of web site.

.CGI

CGI stands for Common Gateway Interface. A .cgi file runs at the Web server and interact with the user via a browser. CGI files can be written using different programming languages, e.g. Perl or C. It works with all browsers, and falls under the category of server-side include.

.PL

This extension indicates a Perl file. It works with all browsers, and falls under the category of server-side include.

.JS

A .js file is a JavaScript file. This file runs at user-end on browser itself.

.JSP

JSP stands for Java Server Page. JSP Pages contain scripts, which are run on server end. It works with all browsers, and falls under the category of server-side include.

.ASP

ASP stands for Active Server Page. ASP provides database connectivity to a web server, and run on server side. ASP scripts can run on IIS Web Server. It works with all browsers, and falls under the category of server-side include.

.PHP or .PHP3
PHP is a content management scripting language, mostly used for Linux or Unix based Web servers. It works with all browsers, and falls under the category of server-side include.

Internet Services in India

Internet Service Providers (ISP)

Internet Service Provider's (ISP) work is to provide Internet connectivity to a user. The user may be an individual or a corporate company.

ISPs serve large companies by providing a high bandwidth direct connection to the Internet. ISPs themselves are connected to one another through their gateways. We can broadly classify ISPs into two categories; one provides basic services, while second category provides value-added services e.g. IT solutions. Typically, for a particular access fee, the service provider provides installation software, a username - password and an access phone number. Most of the ISPs, use Unix (or Linux) computers for several technical reasons.

Types of ISPs in India

Depending upon the type of coverage of geographic area and number of customers, broadly speaking there are two types of ISP present in the Market. All ISP's charge for their services and Internet connectivity whether it is government agency or it is a private company. Due to heavy competition in the market, many ISPs started shakeout processes, changed their service offerings and business models in the recent years. The trend in the industry is of polarisation resulting into a few large ISPs at the national level, and many local ISPs at the regional or local level. Another outcome is increased difficulty to survive, for medium level ISPs .

National ISPs

These ISPs operate at national level and have various points of presence (POP) throughout the country. The distinctive feature is wide coverage. There may be two sub-categories. Examples are ERNET and VSNL.

One category of national ISPs owns the essential network backbone and leases the international connectivity while the other category ISP's taken the lease from other such big ISPs.

Obviously, the main target for these ISPs is the corporate. ISPs owning the network backbone claim the reliability of service (due to ownership of the network) and get a big piece of the cake.

Regional And Local ISPs

These are the ISPs which don't operate on national level instead they usually operate in within a limited geographic region such as smaller towns or particular states. These ISPs serve both the corporate and individual retail consumer segments. They target retail segment users.

Latest Status

Numerous public cyber-cafes are available in our cities and towns. A recent news item says that The National Association for the Blind, India (NAB) in association with Microsoft has launched a Special Cyber Cafe even for the visually impaired in New Delhi. These Cyber-Cafes are doing exactly the same thing for Internet connectivity for the masses, what PCO booths have already done for telephone calls.

ISPs have invested a lot in the last few years; it is well known that the Internet industry in India is in its initial stages and therefore, some of the ISPs are still struggling to get established. At the same time, they are still face the need for continuous investments.

There are many ISPs in India at this time. Currently, there are approximately 400 plus ISP licensees. According to the Department of Telecommunications (DoT), about 437 ISP licenses were given out by the end of 2000. The shakeout and consolidation / mergers of ISPs have been seen in the last two-three years. The major players are ERNET, VSNL, DOT, BSNL and some other Companies such as Satyam Online, HCL Infinet, Mantra OnLine, GNFC Online etc.

An association known as Internet Service Providers Association of India (ISPAI) also exists and has its own website at www.ispai.com. One of the objectives of ISPAI is to achieve and exceed the Planning Commission objective of 230 lakhs Internet Connections by the year 2007. Guidelines to ISPs are also available at www.ispai.com/guidelines.html

Retail Segment

Retail Segment generally refers to Dial-up users. In the retail segment, the first observation is that the competition is tough and revolves around to price or package offered to customers. The only way to compete is by reaching more and more customers; this has been at the centre of policy of ISPs in the retail segment. The Value-added services are absent in this segment. Factors affecting includes mainly two things- fall in access costs and improvement in access to Internet.

Corporate Segment

As most of the corporate companies use the Internet to support important business applications, their focus is on services rather than the costs incurred while obtaining the connectivity. From ISP point of view, "Corporate customers" are easy to retain. Therefore, a good track record for

ISP and list of famous corporate as their customers, are essential to get business from other corporate companies. Some of the Value Added Services provided By ISPs to the corporate clients are listed below:

i. Web Hosting- In this case, Web Server is hosted at ISP's Computer Systems.

ii. IT Solutions- This is an advance offering from ISP than Web Hosting. For Example, It may envelope E-Commerce Solutions for a business firm.

iii. Virtual Private Network (VPN)- A VPN structure, it's access mode and connectivity is provided by ISP to Main Office and remote employees / offices.

iv. Voice Over Internet (VoIP)- This is another case of advance offering like Video-conferencing.

v. E-mail- In this type of service offering, the Email-Server of ISP stores the client firm's emails. It is a very suitable solution for small businesses.

According to Jesse Berst, Editorial Director ZDNet AnchorDesk "The best place to get information about an ISP is from a friend. Find out what their experience has been and if it sounds good take your list of questions to the company and start grilling".

ISP Policy of Govt of India

The ISP Policy was announced in November 98. The ISP Licenses are being issued starting from 6.11.98 on non-exclusive basis. Private ISPs are permitted to setup their own gateways. ISPs are allowed to set up international gateways using satellite and submarine cable landing stations. Period of license is 15 years. Extension may be granted at the discretion of Telecom authority. License fee is waived upto 31.10.2003 and will be Re. 1/- per annum thereafter for those ISPs who obtain licenses prior to 01.11.2003.

(a) Any Indian company with a maximum foreign equity of 74% is eligible (100% is also allowed, but in that case the ISP can not set up an International Gateway).

(b) Based on Service Area of Operation, they are categorized as Category 'A', 'B' and 'C'.

(c) An applicant company may be granted any number of licenses and there will be no limit of number of licenses granted in a particular area.

(d) Performance Bank Guarantee - Rs. 20

Million for Category 'A' Service Area, Rs. 2 Million for each Category 'B' Service Area and Rs. 0.3 Million for each Category 'C' Service Area. (e) ISP can provide Internet Telephony service after obtaining clearance for the same. (f) Exit policy for ISPs has also been finalized.
Category **Service Area**
Category "A" Whole of India
Category "B" 20 territorial Telecom Circles, four Metro Districts- Delhi, Mumbai, Calcutta or Chennai and four major Telephone Districts- Ahmedabad, Bangalore, Hyderabad or Pune.
Category "C" Any Secondary Switching Areas (SSA) of DOT with geographical boundaries as on 1.4.98
Source: *Department of Telecommunications, Ministry of Communications & Information Technology, Govt. of India* ***www.dotindia.com/isp/ispindex.htm***

Table 2.3

IP and Domains

Every IP host on the Internet has a distinct IP address and a distinct domain name associated with it. These two distinct labels associated with a Internet host need to be mapped onto each other. A domain name such as "blr.iar.ac.in" should map onto an IP address such as "202.41.127.8". Such a service is provided by the Domain Name System (DNS). The DNS is a set of protocols and databases. The protocols define the syntax and semantics for a query language to ask questions about information located by DNS-style names. The databases are distributed and replicated. There is no dependence on a single central server, and each part of the database is provided in at least two servers.

The allocation of IP addresses and domain names are centrally done. There is a specific registration process involved. The Internet Assigned Numbers Authority (IANA) is the central Internet authority that allocates IP addresses and domain names through the InterNIC. The allocations are either directly done by the InterNIC or by regional delegated centers. The Asia Pacific region is looked by the APNIC.

The top-level domains in the DNS are EDU, COM, GOV, MIL, ORG, INT, and NET, and all the 2-letter country codes from the list of countries in ISO-3166 (Ref Appendix). In other countries, everything is registered under the 2-letter country code, often with some subdivision. For example, in Korea (KR) the second level names are AC for academic community, CO for commercial, GOV for government, and RE for research. India has a top-level domain IN as listed in the ISO-3166. The second level subdomains registered under the IN domain are ERNET for the academic and research network, NIC for the government's network, NET for Internet Service Providers, RES for the research community, AC for the academic community, CO for commercial organisations and GOV for government offices and machinery. The IN domain administration is done by the National Centre for Software Technology, Bombay (domain-reg@sangam.ncst.ernet.in). The IN domain will be solely managed by the Domain Registrar until either the registration activity is delegated to subdomains or there are separate Domain Registrars for each (or a set) of domains.

Source: E C E Department, Indian Institute of Science, Bangalore
http://ece.iisc.ernet.in/innic/domain.info.html

Domains at a Glance:

co.in	--	For Registered Companies/Trademarks/Banks
firm.in	--	For Proprietary Concerns/Partnership

		Firms/Shops/Liaison Offices
ac.in	--	For Academic Community
res.in	--	For Research Institutes
gov.in	--	For Government Organisations
mil.in	--	For Military Establishments
net.in	--	For Internet Service Providers
in	--	For Internet Service Providers
org.in	--	For Non-profit Organisations
ind.in	--	For Individuals
gen.in	--	For General/Miscellaneous Purpose

Table 2.4

Useful URLs

(Used in this chapter and for further reading)

(All Accessed on Nov. 16, 2003)

1. W3 Web site http://www.w3.org
2. http://www.outreach.utk.edu/iei/laap/projects/tutor1.htm
3. http://www.darwinmag.com/learn/curve/column.html?ArticleID=215
4. http://www.howstuffworks.com/vpn1.htm
5. http://computer.howstuffworks.com/modem1.htm
6. http://whatis.techtarget.com/
7. http://www.intrack.com/intranet/index.cfm
8. http://www.icraindia.com/files/flash/20011016flashisp.pdf
9. http://www.voicendata.com/content/ispwatch/default.asp
10. http://www.zdnetindia.com/techzone/networking/stories/33954.html
11. http://www.isoc.org/internet/history/cerf.shtml
12. http://www1.worldcom.com/global/resources/cerfs_up/
13. http://www.ideafinder.com/history/inventors/berners-lee.htm
14. http://www.ibiblio.org/pioneers/lee.html
15. http://www.ibiblio.org/pioneers/media/vint_www.ram
16. http://www.itprc.com/
17. http://netforbeginners.about.com/
18. Matisse's Glossary of Internet Terms http://www.matisse.net/files/glossary.html
19. Real Player http://www.real.com
20. Acrobat Reader http://www.adobe.com

21. Quicktime player http://quicktime.apple.com
22. IFLA http://www.ifla.org
23. Introduction to TCP/IP
    http://www.yale.edu/pclt/comm/tcpip.htm
24. Introduction to Networking--Alex Yu
    http://seamonkey.ed.asu.edu/~alex/teaching/network/TCPIP.html
25. Teaching tips - Uses for Email Discussion Lists
    http://teaching.polyu.edu.hk/t5/t5c1.asp?topic=5&subtopicid=c
26. Web Reference http://www.webreference.com

CHAPTER 3

Various Information Resources

Knowledge is of two kinds. We know a subject ourselves, or we know where we can find information upon it."

--Samuel Johnson

The Internet is a mix of various sites- Web sites, FTP sites, Telnet Hosts, Discussion sites, etc... As we know that business, libraries, banks, organisations have their web sites, we have to accept that WWW is a popular method of information dissemination and the web supersedes everything. And today it has expanded and mushroomed into a phenomenal resource and proved its competence. There are drawbacks, though. There may not be accurate information to believe; in fact false contents may exist. (There has been a proliferation of Cyber-Nations, which of course are cyber-scams; some of the fake nations have no land at all). However, it would also wrong to imply that all information on the Web is false.

Taking some liberty and considering the popularity of Web sites, we may assume that researchers will be using WWW for most of their work related to research, by either using IE or Netscape.

There are people who believe in communication as integral part of research & view the Internet as nothing but a communication medium & for them everything is communication. The success of free email accounts and chat services, such as Yahoo messenger, ICQ, Humanity etc substantiate the view Internet.

For those, who think of Internet as a source of information:- Web can be viewed as a large collection of libraries worldwide. In this concept, a Web document can be thought of as a 'book', a URL can be thought of as the 'accession number' in the accession register of a library, and a search engine as a helpful 'librarian'. They view the Internet as a massive, unorganised library and they even see communication as content.

Many researchers need to be technically adept, these days and it is the same case with many librarians. There's no question about the traditional print resources (even if their online versions are available), but as a matter of fact Internet has become one popular destination for students and researchers.

To locate the *right information* and retrieve it using a browser, we must know some key searching concepts, before we really start searching for our queries.

For a general reader, some useful Web Resources such as Web sites of Search Engines, Online

References, Libraries, Newspapers, and Govt Information are listed in the Table 3.1 and Table 3.2 as sample.

Search Engines		**Online References**	
Google	Infoseek	Info Please	Dictionary.com
Yahoo	Metacrawler	INFOMINE	Encyclopedia Britannicca
Altavista	ZapMeta	Open Directory	Internet Almanac
Ask Jeeves	Profusion	RefDesk	Roget's Thesaurus
HotBot	Dogpile	Merriam Webster's Online Dictionary	Ask Eric
Lycos	Ixquick		
	Vivisimo		

Table 3.1 A listing of sample of Internet Research Sources websites

Information sources available on WWW

Information sources available on WWW include Chat Rooms, Web Sites, Web Pages, E-Groups, Subject Directories, Live Databases and Web Catalogues. Discussion Forums are an added flavor to all this.

Search Engines are the focal point of all these information resources. And in fact, search engines can itself be treated as information source itself. We will briefly discuss all these types of resources, and later we will explore different ways to find specific information using these sources.

Online Libraries	Online Newspapers	Online Govt. Information
British Council Library India	Web Dunia	Indian Rail
IIT Bombay	Rajasthan Patrika	Income Tax India
DRTC Digital Library	Dainik Bhaskar	NIC
Archieves of Indian Labour Digital Library	The Times of India	UPSC
Questia	The Indian Express	UGC
Internet Public Library	Rediff	BSNL
The Library of Congress	The Hindu	VSNL
Project Guttenberg	The Tribune	NCST
VLib: WWW Virtual Library	Sanjevani	CBSE
Argus ClearingHouse	Malayalam Manorama	ONGC
	Gujarat Samachar	Punjab National Bank
	The Week	Indian-Airlines
		Department of IT
		UNESCO

Table 3.2 Another sample listing of Internet search Resources.

E-Groups

In this book, we will use term "e-group" to refer to various electronic discussion groups. An e-group can be of mainly three types:

Mailing List

Usenet News

Web based Discussion Forum

The mailing list style of discussion operates through email; the newsgroup is like a public bulletin board and operates through its own network called Usenet. The newsgroups are rapidly being replaced by Web based Discussion Forums, which most people used to call as Bulletin Board Systems (some years ago).

Mailing List:- As suggested by its name, these types of e-group are managed through group emails.

We might be remember the concept of the 'journal' grown out of the practice of a 'diary' where scientists/researchers left their notes and comments, and the journals later got printed and distributed among the readers. Mailing list is a type of electronic distribution of a topic-update through e-mail. As we know that email has become very popular among the academics in late 80's, thus leading to popularity of the concept of Mailing List. The person who has created the mailing list is known as the owner of the mailing list; the mailing list may be moderated or unmoderated. In an unmoderated list, the topic-update is distributed to all members of the list through email automatically, while in a moderated list posts are filtered through a moderator who must approve/edit messages before distributions.

Mailing -list type of e-groups are often moderated and happen to be professional in nature, and are created by associations and organisations to serve a user community.

Many mailing lists are not meant for discussion, and are meant for announcement type. Some of them are used by webmasters for newsletters and notices etc.

One key feature of Mailing Lists is that they tend to be more scholarly and professional in content comparing to Usenet newsgroups.

Usenet News: - Very soon, Newsgroups will be a thing of the past, as these are replaced swiftly by Web based Discussion forums and bulletin boards. Newsgroup networks form an e-group and are considered a useful information resource. Unlike Mailing List, there is no subscription needed, and anyone can post in newsgroups. Newsgroups are well known for grassroots views.

By subscribing to a newsgroup you can get following information:

Find people who have expertise in a field.

Contacts details of people with similar interests.

Answer of your question.

Get references to other sources of related information.

One can read news using newsreader program, which is included in browsers or one can use Outlook Express or Incredimail as an alternative to access to Usenet network.

Discussion Forums:- Being a member of a Discussion Forum is an activity for knowledge-building on a subject topic. There are a large number of discussion groups available representing a vast array of interests. These forums help people use the Internet to make a difference. Though many Discussion forums boards look different, all of them function pretty much the same way. Each forum is divided into various topics. When you choose a topic, you see a collection of or views questions.

Linked to each question are many answers or replies people have posted on the board. People can share the thoughts, views, and files using these Discussion Groups.

Since, these are web-based and multi-threaded, you can follow a thread from its beginning all the way to the latest answer, unraveling the discussion in the order it occurred.

In other words, you don't have to be present when a discussion occurs--it takes place over a period of time. You can get a lot of information and answers for your queries.

Example: *Experts-exchange.com* is a popular discussion forum among IT professionals.

Directories	These are nothing more than organised lists.

Like the yellow pages of a telephone directory, one can find information by browsing through a list of topics in a directory. An example is Yahoo directory (www.yahoo.com).

Another example is 'open directory project' shown in Fig 3.1, in which you can observe various sub-topics listed under a wide subject topic arranged in a hierarchical fashion.

These are lists of carefully selected Internet sites, or resources collected and organised by humans and not by computers. The editors do the work, select sites for inclusion in their directories only after a review on some selection criteria.

Directories tend to be smaller than search engine databases, typically indexing top level pages of a site.

Portals are directories that have been created (or taken over) by commercial groups. Portals also offer additional services (emails, news, maps etc...).

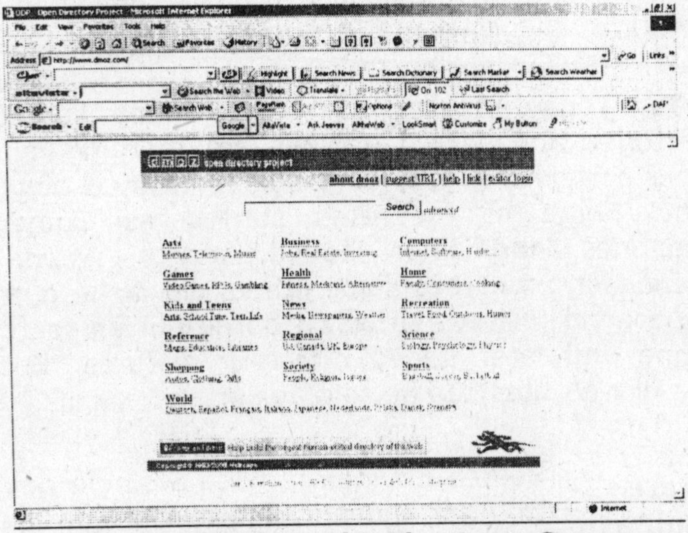

Fig. 3.1 Example of a Directory: Open Directory Project website

Advantages:

Have the capabilities of delivering a higher quality content.

Provide less irrelevant results in comparison to results from search engines.

Subject directories are best for browsing and for topic of more general type.

Disadvantages:

Dead links are real problems for subject directories. While in comparison, search engines do not struggle with such problems as they have the capability to automatically remove dead links from theirdatabase.

NOTE: Today, as per the trend, many subject directories and search engines are merging in a single portal site, providing search form a single point. Some of the sites started as Subject Directories and later added *search engine's functionality;* whereas some others did it the other way around (in reverse way); borne out as search engine and later added d*irectory features.* Both type of web sites can be said as portals.

Search Engines

Search Engines provide a single point to find relevant information on any topic. As you may well be aware 'Relevance is the Holy Grail of search', elusive yet crucial. Search Engines are good for finding relevant information on distinctive or obscure topics, provided that searcher knows some unique term to which will be found in the pages, searcher desire. Intelligent guessing can help someone to find right results.

Tool 3.1

Search Engines can search the whole of web and bring you the required documents. However, no search engine is capable to search what you want, so you have to find some specific keyword and apply some Boolean logic in order to search for your query. An example of a popular search engine is Ask Jeeves (www.ask.com).

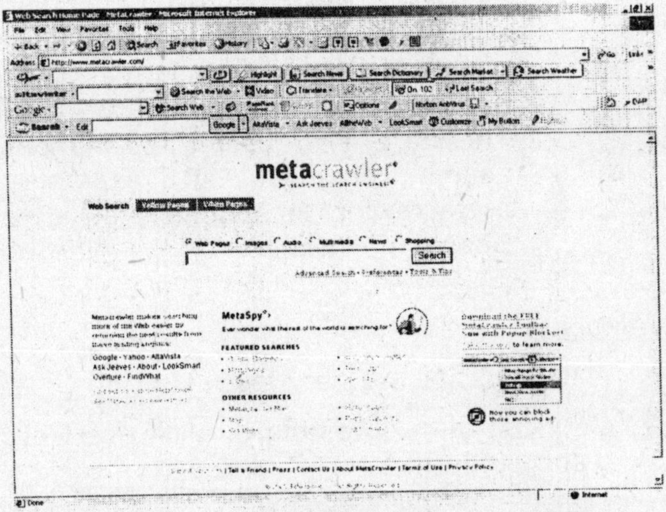

Fig. 3.2 Example of a meta search engine website: metacrawler.com

Meta Search Engines

Metasearch engines do not crawl the web for compiling their own searchable databases. Instead, they take a different approach and act intelligent by searching the databases of multiple sets of individual search engines simultaneously, from a single site and using the same interface.

Metasearches provide a quick way of finding out which engines are retrieving the best results for you in your search. Meta-Search Engines search simultaneously in many search engines and provide some results. They are also useful for comparing search engines. An example is metacrawler (www.metacrawler.com) Shown in Fig. 3.2

Advantages:

1. Metasearches are very fast.
2. Very useful in obtaining a quick overview on a subject term.

Disadvantages:

Metasearch engines do not offer the options that individual search engines usually provide.

You are dependent on metasearch engine as far as how the search is configured and conducted, only a few options can be configured by user and to some extent only.

The speed is also slower comparing with Search Engines.

Gateways Gateways can be of two types: *library gateways* and *portals.*

Library gateways are collections of databases and informative sites, arranged subject-wise, assembled, reviewed and recommended by specialists, (usually librarians). These gateway support research and reference needs by identifying and pointing to recommended, academically-oriented pages on the Web.

Use of library gateways is appreciated when you are looking for high quality information on the Web. You can be assured about the quality of contents of these sites as have been reviewed and evaluated fairly by subject specialists for their accuracy.

Examples of some Library Gateways

Academic Information Acedemic Information web site is running on web address www.academicinfo.net is quite good for basic research. It is an annotated subject directory of resources. Resources are categorised in 3 sections:

- Subject Gateways
- Reference Desk

- Student Centre

Digital Librarian

www.digital-librarian.com is a popular source for information on various topics listed on the web site. It is a web site maintained by Margaret Vail Anderson, a librarian in Cortland, New York. Many people such as teachers, lawyers, writers etc. use this site for reference purposes.

The site appears to be updated on a regular basis. Each page has a search link to Amazon.com. Each resource page includes the date on which it was checked last time.

INFOMINE

INFOMINE (http://infomine.ucr.edu) is a recognised virtual library due to the contribution of librarians.

The collection has links to many useful e-resources such as databases, e-journals, e-books, bulletin boards, online library card catalogues, mailing lists, articles, directories of researchers, and many other types of information and is relevant to students, researchers, faculty at university level.

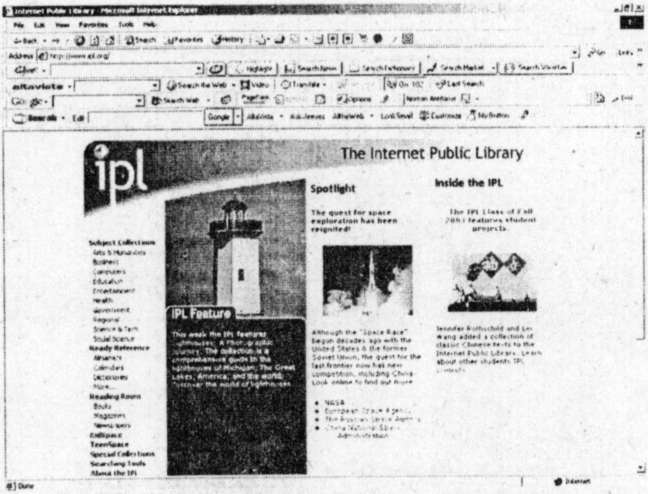

Fig. 3.3 Example of Library Gateway: Internet Public Library (ipl.org)

Internet Public Library (IPL)

As shown in Fig. 3.3, the Internet Public Library is a public service organisation and a learning/teaching environment at the University of Michigan School of Information and its web site is running on www.ipl.org/.

Through the IPL, librarians and library students learn to integrate the use of the Internet into their professional practice and others find help in order to find out the desired resources from the gigantic web.

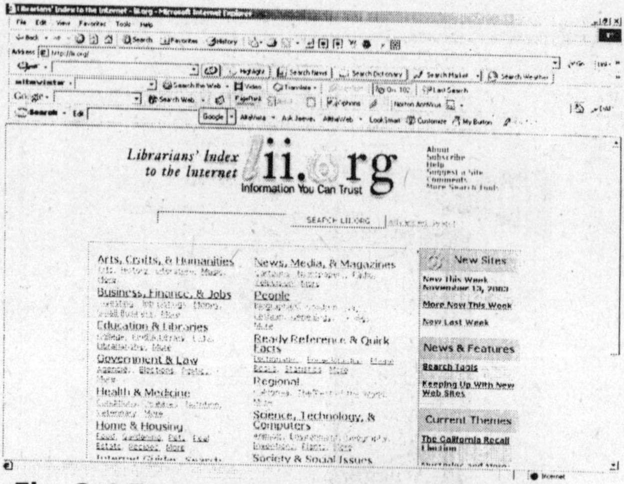

Fig. 3.4 Example of a Library Gateway: Librarian's Index to the Internet (lii.org)

Librarians' Index to the Internet

The Librarians' Index to the Internet (lii.org) is a searchable, annotated subject directory of more than 12,000 Internet resources selected and evaluated by volunteer librarian indexers from throughout California & other places in USA and is shown in Fig. 3.4.

Both librarians and end-users can use the Index, as a quick and efficient tool for locating authoritative, reliable information on the Web. Quality of their resources is quite good, as they contain less erroneous or dead links.

Subject-Specific Databases Subject-specific databases, or vortals (i.e., "vertical portals") are databases devoted to a single subject, created by subject specialists.

Most progressive practitioners like to use subject-specific databases when they are looking for information on a specific topic or subject. For some subjects thousands of databases may exist and devoted to specific topics of interest may be found after some research.

Examples of some Subject-Specific Databases

Subject	Site Name	Web Address
Movies	Internet Movie Database	http://us.imdb.com
Educational Information	Ask ERIC	www.askeric.org/
Sports	SportSearch	www.sportssearch.com
Travelling	• Expedia • Out Look Traveller	www.expedia.com www.outlooktraveller.com
Jobs	• Monster • CareerAge • Naukari • Careers India	www.monsterindia.com www.careearage.com www.naukari.com www.careersindia.com
Psychology	PsychCrawler	www.psychcrawler.com

Health	• Med India •IndiaMedical Info •IndiaDoctors • WebMD	www.medindia.net www.indiamedicalinfo.com www.indiadoctors.org www.webmd.com

Table 3.3

Invisible Web

"Invisible Web" or the "Deep Web" (accounting for 60 to 80 percent of existing Web material) includes, password-protected sites, documents behind firewalls, archived material, interactive tools, and the contents of certain databases. Sites providing web –enabled databases falls under this category.

These type of resources are not usually visible to search engine spiders. In order to access so-called "Invisible Web" sites, you have to point your browser directly at them. That's what many library gateways and subject-specific databases do. They are good sources for direct links to database information stored on the "Invisible Web." More details can be found in the later section of this chapter.

Virtual Libraries

The 'Libraries without walls' is a slogan sentence. Vlib is an Example and shown in Fig. 3.5

The virtual digital library, a concept that is quickly becoming a reality, offers rapid and geography-independent access to text, images, graphics, motion video and other datatypes.

Fig. 3.5 Example of Virtual Library: vlib.org

Different ways to find information

There are a number of basic ways to access information on the Internet:

1. By joining an e-group
2. By exploring classified subject directories (also called classified subject gateways)

3. By Searching through a search engine (or Metasearch Engine)

4. By exploring the "deep Web" (i.e. live databases on the Web)

5. By exploring Virtual Libraries.

In this Chapter, we will be focusing on the Search Engines, Classified Directories that are also known as Subject Gateways, and Deep Web also known as Invisible Web. The rest of the methods are left to the reader as an exercise.

Joining an e- group

There are many active discussion groups also known as e-groups or discussion forums (such as yahoo groups on http://groups.yahoo.com) available on the Internet covering a range of topics. Nmlis, employmentlaws_India, UGC_NET_CS, INDIA-FORCE, are some of the examples of yahoo groups discussing about library and information science, employment laws, UGC NET Exam for computer science discipline, Agriculture librarianship respectively.

You can ask questions to experts and read the answers to questions asked by others. Belonging to these e-groups helps you enhance knowledge for some specific topic and other relevant areas. Software programs Listserv, Listproc, and

Majordomo are used to manage e-mail discussion groups on a. server machine. Yahoo Groups (groups.yahoo.com) and MSN groups (groups.msn.com) are very popular e-groups worldwide. Usenet newsgroups can be accessed using a newsreader program. E-mail Client programs such as outlook express or browsers such as Netscape have inbuilt newsreader functionality.

While some forums are simple bulletin Board, others are email discussion groups.

A sample post in one library related Indian Bulletin-Board System (**IndLibra**) is being given below as an example:

> Date: 10-31-03 04:58
>
> Dear Friends,
>
> Few days back there was lot of debate on this forum to have a database of Indian Librarians [Information Professionals]. Then there was one solution, which basically was very near to an On-Line Bulletin Board/ Forum.
>
> Just to check out what all it takes to start an On-Line Bulletin / Forum. I created an Bulletin Board/Forum at http://indlibra.myforum.net . It has been named as IndLIBRA. It is for discussion among Indian Librarians and Inforamtion Scientists.
>
> Can you guess how much time it might have

taken!!!? It was done with in 10 Minutes!!!. No prizes for guessing it right. This 10 minutes also includes getting a Yahoo email account (which I will never use!!), was given to register for the free Forum.

Check out http://indlibra.myforum.net and have fun. Create your own such discussion forums and enjoy your creativity. BUT WAIT, NEVER GIVE YOUR REAL EMAIL for such fun.

NOW DO NOT ASK ME HOW MUCH IT TAKES TO ESTABLISH A FORUM (not start). IT IS VERY VERY DIFFICULT!!!.

Regards
Sukhdev Singh

Source: http://indlibra.myforum.net/read.php3?id=2

Examples of some E – Groups

WBTOLL-L WBTOLL-L is an email discussion group, which discusses Web Based Training (WBT) and related issues. High quality discussions can be found there. To subscribe, you can send an e-mail message to listserv@hermes.circ.gwu.edu with the command: signon WBTOLL-L in the body of the message. If you send an email to the above email address, it will be delivered to all the members of the list. It's archive is available at http://hermes.circ.gwu.edu/archives/wbt

oll-l.html.

LIS-Forum Another example of mailing list, which is very popular among Library and Information Science professional is run by NCSI, located in IISC, Bangalore. You can send an email to LIS-Forum@ncsi.iisc.ernet.in, and it will be delivered to all the members of the list. It's archive is available at http://ncsi.iisc.ernet.in/mailman/listinfo/lis-forum

Exploring a classified subject directory

The numbers of Classified Subject directories are increasing on WWW. As already discussed these directories are organised subject-wise and consist of links to Internet resources relating to these subjects and are created by either institutions or by volunteers. The major subject directories available on the Web tend to have overlapping (but have different) contents. Most directories provide a search capability too, that allows you to query the database on your topic of interest.

INFOMINE, from the University of California, is a good example of an academic subject directory.

Yahoo has a very famous commercial directory structure.

Search engines and searching techniques

Search engines may search Internet or Intranet files, locally-mounted databases, files on your own computer desktop, image databases, multimedia databases or any other kind of computer-readable files.

There are search engines we can use for our Intranet web site; (e.g. Microsoft's Site Server). In this section of the book, we are focusing on web search engines such as Google, Yahoo, AltaVista, Teoma etc. So term Search Engine will refer here to Web Search Engine (portal sites).

Search engines are located on the World Wide Web due to two main reasons, one is the popularity of HTTP Protocol and second the user-friendliness of browsers, as indicated by the fact that browsers have established themselves as standard GUI window for WWW.

Many search engines compile a database spanning multiple Internet protocols, including HTTP, FTP, and Usenet. Often accessible as separate portion of searches, some of them (such as AltaVista) contain the capability to search (multimedia or other file types) the deep web.

Generally speaking, a Web search engine service consists of three components:

- **Spider or crawler or robot:** It is a program that traverses the Web from link to link, identifying and reading pages using *Breadth-First-Search algorithm*. By following the breadth-first algorithm a crawler or spider ensures that it is not lost in the depth of a Binary Search Tree.

Spider has some limitations also. Searching for data from databases from the web is not possible for a spider as data stored in relational databases is ordinarily accessed using queries structured to match the table structure and organisation of the database. In addition, a spider cannot enter into private secured area of web sites.

- **Indexing part:** It is a relational database containing a copy of each Web page provided by the crawler. Indexing multimedia (Audio & Video) is much more complex than indexing text. In some cases the media needs to be converted to text.

- **Presentation part of Search engine mechanism:** It is a program that enables users to query the database and returns results in an (relevancy ranked) order on the web.

  Search programs cannot search from inside the audio or video clips, as video indexing and retrieval is a tougher job for these programs. A few existing web search engines can find some video clips, with limited results of those Web pages with text that can be searched by keywords.

Spiders are indiscriminate and unintelligent too, as some of the collected resources may be outdated. However, search engines have the capabilities to detect dead links, but that is not enough. Therefore, you have to be sure to evaluate the search results.

New generation search engines offer improved ranking of results. A new development in search engine technology is the ordering of search results by concept, keyword, site, links or popularity.

Query Formulation

All search engines have their own rules for formulating queries. It is obvious that you should read the help section at the site, before beginning the search to get right information.

Learn the art of formulation of your query by Identifying your concepts by narrow down your topic into its component concepts and listing keywords for each concept and finally specifying the logical relationships among your keywords. Since every search engine provides a different syntax to write down the queries using different set of operators for Boolean logic, you have to first master the art of formulating query for the respective search engine. Also to recommend is to read the section 'Advance' on search engine web site.

Boolean Operators

Logical relationships imply Boolean logic.

There are three main logical operators: **AND, OR, NOT.** If the exact phrase is to be searched then it should be written in quotes, such as if you want to search for Operation Parakram, then you should write is as "Operation Parakram".

Using Boolean expressions, you can limit your results to very specific information. You may also use parentheses in Boolean searches to create complex Boolean expressions. There are + and – sign also available. If you require some words or phrases to appear (or not) in your search results, you can use a + sign or - sign before that word or phrase that you **must** or **must not** have. Then, again there is a % sign to replace a single letter in a word. This is useful for words that have different regional spellings, or which are commonly misspelled (for example: you can write/ search for organi%e as organize or organise depending upon your language.).

There is * sign for replacing many characters in a word, for example you can use * for jay* for jaymal or jayant.

Search Statement	Result of search
(first word)AND (last word)	both these terms
(first word) OR (last word)	at least one of these terms

first NOT last	the term first but not last
" This is a phrase"	exact phrase
First word -second	first word but not second

Take a look at the results. If you are not finding what you want, repeat the search with alternative keywords. Your initial results may give you ideas about which new terms to try. Include synonyms or alternate spellings in your search statements and connect these terms with OR logic. Exclude unwanted term by using minus(-).

Experiment with different search engines. No two search engines work from the same index. Use vocabulary that is specific to your topic; avoid words with large concepts unless you intend to field search.

Link appropriate terms with the Boolean AND (+) so that each term is required to appear in the record. If you have too few results: then Drop off the least important concept(s) to broaden your subject and use more general vocabulary. Add alternate terms or spellings for individual concepts and connect with the Boolean OR.

Some engines also add Near, FAR and BEFORE as other types of Boolean operators.

Similarities in Search Engines

All search engines are different but have some commonalities. They do have. Few similarities are very clear:

1. As shown in Tool 3.1, somewhere on their Web page is a place (text box) to enter the topic you are looking for. There is a text box available in which you can type the word or phrase and there is a button too, either displayed as go or search. (You click the search button to find the desired results).

2. The working philosophy is the same. Search engines are websites that automatically document information available on the web in form of a updateable relational database. We search through this database. Search Engine responds to the query of a researcher by looking through its database and displaying all the matching sites.

3. All the search engines like to take input from webmasters to promote their sites.

4. No search engine can search the entire web (as the size of WWW is too large).

Differences in Search Engines

There are many search engines available, and they differ on many criteria, some are mentioned below:

1. Difference in *Grouping of results:* Search engines group (cluster) all results that come

from a single web site together, displaying only one of them in the results listing and also providing "More Pages..." or a similar message. Grouping will differ with each search engine.

2. Difference in *Nested Search:* While some search engine may allow you to "Search within these results" and to narrow down your results by performing a nested search; there are others, which don't provide this feature.
3. Difference in *Site descriptions:* Different search engines provide different text against query. Often the text given is simply the first words in the site, which may or may not accurately indicate the site's content or quality.
4. Difference in *Other format Searching:* While some search engines provide search facility for image formats and MS-office file formats, others don't.
5. Some search engines are primary search-providers while others may be users of these primary search providers.

Deep Web

There are some web sites, which can search in Deep web. As mentioned here, Deep web refer to the online database in public domain for public usage. Crawlers (or Spiders) cannot access the data values stored in the live relational databases residing on the web, because of their inability to extract content from databases.

Other types of content, which form the invisible web, include non-text proprietary formats such as PPT, PDF, and Multimedia files. Till date only few search engines provide to search something from these types of files, Google is one of those which integrates PDF and MS-Office files searching with its general searching feature. Google not only supports Unicode, translate from one language to other but also can search in Unicode supported language contents.

The only way to access information on the invisible Web (such as INFLIBNET Databases) is to search the databases themselves. Database information may include anything such as news, job advertisements, various time schedules or any dynamically changing information or even video files.
Some of the sites providing peeping into invisible web are mentioned below:

Invisible-web.net http://www.invisible-web.net/
Search.Com http://www.search.com/
Complete Planet http://www.completeplanet.com
Resource Discovery Network http://www.rdn.ac.uk

A Comparison

A Search Engine is accessed by a web site; providing the user a text box to type something and press Enter on go (or find or search) button, to search several matching results. In fact, Search engines are huge databases (of web page files). Search Engines are built of several components, "Spider" or "robots" or "crawler" get a web site, they typically index most of the words on the publicly available pages on a site, moving from link to link, identifying and perusing pages. A site with no links to other web page will be missed by spiders.Usually search engines index the full-text of a web page, so a lot of information is held in their databases. A user, most probably the Webmaster can submit a site to a search engine to crawl the links and pages, for inclusion in their database. One of the jobs of crawler is to develop the database by filling the links and description of the link. When we try to find out some of the information from the search engine website, the presentation part of search engine finds from its database, produces the most relevant results, and provides us the set of hyperlinks.

Search Engines can be classified into two broad categories, one is normal, and the other is metasearch. While normal search engines compile their own searchable databases on the web; the other category Metasearch engines, do not develop their own databases. Instead, they normally search the databases of other search engines (search the databases of individual search engines) at a time, by firing queries to many search engines. Some of the metaserach engines also give the option to user to choose their preferred search engines, to whom query should be sent to.

When to use a normal (individual) search engine such as google, and when to use a metasearch engine such as profusion and when to use a classified directory such as Yahoo, and when to find from invisible web, such as INFLIBNET is the sole decision of the researcher, who think appropriate.

However, some points can be noted such as: metasearch engines will produce few results but relevant results for your query, because whole web thus limiting the number of results retrieved. In addition, some metasearch engines (e.g.Go2Net) another example will cluster results, meaning that if a particular resource is found in more than one search engine, it will be listed only once. However, even if metasearch engines are a good way to retrieve rare resources, using a metasearch engine can help to cover more part of web to search, due to reduction in the overlapping results from different search engines.

While classified directories offer the tree structure and grouping of topics, under the umbrella of a broader subject, enabling you to see individual resources, they may miss some of the site, if the human editor forgot to add (or delete). A classified directory can usually be used in two ways: you can browse through the subject hierarchies, or you can search by keyword very much similar to searching in a search engine.

You can browse through almost like looking for a book in a library shelf; the individual resources have been grouped under one directory. When you go for searching mode, remember that you are searching only the catalogue cards only, created by someone, say cataloguer and not the WWW as search engines do.

However, if your key words are found in a resource's catalogue record you may find a relevant resource. Classified directories usually have higher relevancy than search engines, because some other human being, who found them relevant, has already judged them. Classified directories are a good place to start if you want to browse in a particular subject area.

A subject gateway is nothing, but simply a classified directory for a specific subject e.g. chemistry. Librarians who are subject specialists run many subject gateways and use existing classification systems to evaluate web resources. Information gateways generally contain fewer resources than a general search engine.

The process of finding relevant resources for a serious research on the Internet has therefore become more complicated. Once you have defined what you are looking for, you may go to find that type of information, but evaluation of such information would be required.

EVALUATING WEB PAGES

Since pages of web site are more dynamic & rate of updation (changing) is more; there fore, due to these changes, web pages may be outdated, inaccurate or incomplete, thus not fitting to the requirement of a researcher. Therefore, one who wishes to use Internet as a source of information requires evaluation of web pages. The broad criteria for evaluation is based upon the targeted section of audience, source of information, accuracy of contents & some of them are listed below for reader's help; however, evaluation of web resource is an art and can be learnt only by practice.

Jim Kapoun a reference and instruction librarian at Southwest State University, writes in his article entitled " *Teaching undergrads WEB evaluation: A guide for library instruction*" (in C&RL News, July/August 1998 Volume 59 No. 7) that "*I base Web evaluation on five criteria that I use for print evaluation: accuracy, authority, objectivity, currency, and coverage....*

Accuracy- If your page lists the author and institution that published the page and provides a way of contacting him/her

Authority-If your page lists the author credentials and its domain is preferred (.edu, .gov, .org, or .net), and. . .

Objectivity- If your page provides accurate information with limited advertising and it is objective in presenting the information, and . . .

Currency- If your page is current and updated regularly (as stated on the page) and the links (if any) are also up-to-date, and . . .

Coverage- If you can view the information properly—not limited to fees, browser technology, or software requirement, then . . .

You may have a higher quality Web page that could be of value to your research! "

Ellen Chamberlen, (from University of South Carolina) even suggests *assessing the stability of web pages* in USC Beufort Library Tutorial BareBones:101, in his own words as: *"There is no way to freeze a web page in time. Unlike the print world with its publication dates, editions, ISBN numbers, etc., web pages are fluid. There's no bibliographic control on the web. The page you cite today may be altered or revised tomorrow, or it might disappear completely. The page owner might or might not acknowledge the changes and, if he relocates the page, might or might not leave a forwarding address. Try to assess the stability of the pages you reference. Again, one of the best ways to do this is to look closely at the page sponsor, last date updated, and the authority of the author(s). When you are writing a paper and using web pages as source material, keep a backup of what you find on the web, (either as a printout or saved to disk) so that you can verify your sources later on if need be.* "

The Librarians / Information Scientists should be able to help a researcher by offering their expertise in evaluating a web page, and in citation.

Mainly you need to check for the authenticity of the publisher (or author) and validity of contents. You need to train your eyes and fingers to raise the objections, to filter out and to not consider irrelevant or suspicious contents.

SOURCE

Whether Author is identifiable? Does this work have been already published in a print version? Can anyone find his (or her) identity? Have the e-publisher and author has given their contact information providing email address only is not enough physical address should be there.

Whether author has expertise on the subject discipline? Is he a known figure in that area? Check for credentials in particular subject.

Whether location and address of the site is appropriate / valid (to the material as shown in the URL,) and also referred by lots of other sites of same subject?

Check the perimeter of the page, and try to find out the links such as "About us", "Who am I" etc.

lways search for the author's name in the Search Engine. For Example, if Ram Singh is an author then you can search in Google by typing *Ram Singh* and "*Ram Singh*" or "*Ram * Singh*". Note the different results, and verify from the other sources, cross-verify the sources.

CONTENT

- Check for the accuracy of content, one should not believe the information presented at face value.

- Source of the information should be clearly stated [whether original or borrowed].
- One should use additional print and electronic sources to complement the information you have found on WWW.
- One should check whether links are relevant and appropriate.
- One should look for the "copyright permissions" at the bottom of the page.
- One should be sure to investigate additional sites on the topic
- Browse a reputable subject directory (such as Librarian's Index (Lii.org), About.com, Infomine, and Yahoo etc.) to verify the content. You can even look into Citation Index maintained at web site Web of Science (http://www.webofscience.com).

CITATION ISSUES

These searching concepts on WWW are good & quick methods; but problematic issues are there. First is, quantity and diversity of resources available, is huge; most of the search engines are not able to show the relevant hyperlinks on the first page. Instead they come up with findings of thousands of results, thus increasing the load of problem for a researcher.

At last, when the researcher finds the page, it may be unauthorised and totally faked one. Thus it is difficult to keep track of valuable information. Evaluation is one-way for not becoming a fool. How to evaluate web documents, what are the techniques etc, needs to be known to a researcher; if he is going to take help from web.

Some points are being touched, while others are for readers to explore.

Information sources are changing- New Information comes each day, and in networked environment, the structure of a web site and thus of WWW is constantly changing. Everyday a page may get changed; some new information might be added or some obsolete contents might be removed; there is no way to freeze a web page with respect to time. In print world, there is stability, there are ISBN Numbers, Author, Publication dates, editions etc., but according to the experts, the web pages are fluid, even a hacker can modify a page and thus there is no bibliographic control, and Citation has become a problem, because webmaster can change the page or remove the page the next day you cited.

The page owner or author may be fake, what his intention was to put page on web for public couldn't be guessed. The best way is that to look sharply the page last updated, page author, linked other pages etc. See the domain name of the page, which entity or organisation published it, which type of domain name it is, whether it is .edu or .gov or some private organisation, what is the level of the organisation etc. If it is published in personal capacity then whether that person has the background and qualification to write on that subject and he is not any hobbyist or a pro-claimed author.

Lack of cataloguing- There is no comprehensive listing of all networked resources & no search engine can do this. There is no coverage of all the topics. If you need to search the page, don't forget to search in a search engine by typing hyperlink followed by *site://* in search engine, which provide domain restriction feature (e.g. google). There should be no space after the slashes.

For Example, if you want to search for pages having "Tim Berners Lee" only from the web site of w3.org then you can make your search expression as *"Tim Berners Lee" site://w3.org* , type this expression in Google and press enter.

Uneven Subject coverage- Since, cyberspace is a collection of networked information in form of web pages, therefore, despite the quantity of information, coverage across the range of subjects is still uneven. Generally, the quality of print journal or document shall be higher than the one published in cyberspace, because anybody can publish in cyberspace, while getting an article printed in some reputed scholarly journal will not be that much easy.

Quality control not applied- Generally speaking, the quality of e-resources may be poor. The reason responsible for this is the variation in quality of the information published on the Internet and all those don't necessarily undergo the same assessment as paper publications, specially e-journals which are not equivalent to their print journals. Always look for the publisher of the web site, if that publisher has the same material in print-format, before citing.

CITATIONS OF ELECTRONIC RESOURCES (Samples in APA Style)

New Media for publishing always presents problems and challenges for bibliographers, and they have to either devise or learn the method about citation to maintain bibliographic control. Citation of electronic resources is a new challenge for us. How to cite and what to cite? As you know that there are many styles such as MLA, APA, Old-MLA etc.

It is true that e-resources augment, the print resources. But it is to note that unlike the print, on the Internet, there is no category for unpublished or semi-published material therefore; it means that everything is published on the Internet and by anybody.

Most probably while citing online resources such as web-enabled databases, Internet Sites (WWW, Telnet, Gopher, FTP), web documents etc. We would like to think about them as Books and online communication of emails, discussion groups as Serials. However, citation of e-resources should be minimal in a research work as the reference source can be changed or moved to some other location or deleted without the knowledge of researcher, and citation of electronic resources should be given only when the equivalent work is not published because unlike the published printed work, the electronic work is not fixed with respect to time. Therefore, the references may not prove correct with the elapse of time. Anyway, some sample citations of electronic resources are given below in APA Style in order to help to learn citation of e-resources, (if print work is not available) to some extent and meant for new professionals -

E-mail

1. From e-mail correspondence between J. Wilhite and Lennart Dahlberg, IFLA/ALP, August 28, 2002.

2. From e-mail correspondence between J. Wilhite and Batlang Comma Serema, January 21, 2003.

Electronic Journal

Deutch, J., & Smith, J. H. (2002). Smarter intelligence. *Foreign Policy*, 128, 64-69.

Retrieved August 13, 2002, from ProQuest database.

Electronic NewsPaper

McGee, J. (2001, November 28). Joint task force became model of counterterrorism. *The Washington Post*. Retrieved August 13, 2002, from ProQuest database.

Web Article

Place, Emma 'International collaboration on Internet Subject Gateways' IFLA Journal V26(1)2000 p.52-56.

Workshop Proceeding

Maphatane, M. *Bridging the digital divide: Postal Business Unit. Presentation at the Africa Day Workshop 2001.* Retrieved January 11, 2002 from: http://www.umts-forum.org/presentations/Postal_Policy_and_Postal_Projects.pdf.

Useful URLs
(Used in this chapter and for further reading)

(All Accessed on Nov. 16, 2003)

1. Google Web site http://www.google.com
2. Yahoo Web site http://www.yahoo.com
3. Altavista Web site http://www.altavista.com

4. Lycos Web site http://www.lycos.com
5. Ask Jeeves Web site http://www.ask.com
6. HotBot Web site http://www.hotbot.com
7. Infoseek Web site http://www.infoseek.com
8. Go Web site http://www.go.com
9. Metacrawler Web site http://www.metcrawler.com
10. Profusion Web site http://www.profusion.com
11. Dogpile Web site http://www.dogpile.com
12. Ixquick Web site http://ixquick.com
13. Vivisimo Web site http://www.vivisimo.com
14. Info Please Web site http://www.infoplease.com
15. INFOMINE Web site http://infomine.ucr.edu
16. Open Directory Project http://www.dmoz.com
17. Academic Info Ref Desk http://www.academicinfo.net/ref.html
18. Merriam Webster's Online Dictionary http://www.m-w.com/
19. Dictionary.com Web site http://www.dictionary.com
20. Encyclopedia Britannicca http://www.britannica.com/
21. Internet Almanac http://www.thebird.org/web/almanac.html
22. Roget's Thesaurus http://thesaurus.reference.com/Roget-Alpha-Index.html
23. Thesaurus Web site http://thesaurus.com
24. Ask Eric http://www.askeric.org
25. British Council Library India http://library.britishcouncil.org.in/

26. IIT Bombay http://www.iitb.ac.in
27. DRTC Digital Library http://drtc.isibang.ac.in/gsdl/
28. Archives of Indian Labour Digital Library http://www.indialabourarchives.org/
29. Questia www.questia.com
30. Internet Public Library http://www.ipl.org
31. The Library of Congress http://www.loc.gov
32. Project Guttenberg http://promo.net/pg/
33. VLib: WWW Virtual Library http://vlib.org
34. Argus ClearingHouse http://www.clearinghouse.net/
35. Web Dunia http://www.webdunia.com
36. Rajasthan Patrika http://www.rajasthanpatrika.com
37. Dainik Bhaskar http://www.bhaskar.com
38. The Times of India http://www.indiatimes.com
39. The Indian Express http://www.indian-express.com
40. Rediff http://www.rediff.com
41. The Hindu http://www.hinduonnet.com
42. The Tribune www.tribuneindia.com/
43. Sanjevani http://www.sanjevani.com/
44. Malayalam Manorama www.malayalamanorama.com/
45. Gujarat Samachar http://www.gujaratsamachar.com
46. The Week Daily Update http://www.the-week.com/daily.htm
47. Indian Rail http://www.indianrail.gov.in
48. Income Tax India http://www.incometaxindia.gov.in
49. NIC Web site http://www.nic.in
50. UPSC Web site http://www.upsc.gov.in
51. UGC Web site http://www.ugc.ac.in

52. BSNL Web site http://bsnl.co.in
53. VSNL Web site http://www.vsnl.com
54. NCST Web site http://www.ncst.ernet.in
55. CBSE Web site http://www.cbse.nic.in
56. ONGC Web site http://www.ongcindia.com
57. Punjab National Bank Web site http://pnbindia.com
58. Indian Airlines Web site http://indian-airlines.nic.in
59. Department of Information Technology Web site http://www.mit.gov.in
60. UNESCO Web site http://www.unesco.org
61. Experts-Exchange http://www.experts-exchange.com
62. MetaCrawler Web site http://www.metacrawler.com
63. Digital Librarian http://www.digital-librarian.com
64. Internet Movie Database http://us.imdb.com
65. SportSearch www.sportssearch.com
66. Expedia Web site http://www.expedia.com
67. Out Look Traveller www.outlooktraveller.com
68. Monster www.monsterindia.com
69. CareerAge www.careearage.com
70. Careers India www.careersindia.com
71. Naukari.com www.naukari.com
72. PsychCrawler www.psychcrawler.com
73. Med India www.medindia.net
74. India Medical Info www.indiamedicalinfo.com
75. India Doctors www.indiadoctors.org
76. WebMD www.webmd.com
77. Yahoo Groups Home http://groups.yahoo.com

78. NMLIS http://groups.yahoo.com/nmlis/
79. Employments Laws of India Yahoo Group
    http://groups.yahoo.com/employments_laws/
80. UGC -NET Computer Science
    http://groups.yahoo.com/ugc_net_cs/
81. INDIA FORCE http://groups.yahoo.com/india-force/
82. MSN Groups home http://groups.msn.com
83. INDLIBRA http://indlibra.myforum.net
84. WBTOLL-L
    http://hermes.circ.gwu.edu/archives/wbtoll-l.html
85. LIS-Forum
    http://ncsi.iisc.ernet.in/mailman/listinfo/lis-forum
86. Invisible-web.net http://www.invisible-web.net/
87. Search.Com http://www.search.com/
88. Complete Planet
    http://www.completeplanet.com
89. Resource Discovery Network http://www.rdn.ac.uk
90. http://cas.memphis.edu/~mcrouse/elcite.html
91. http://sunsite.berkeley.edu/Web4Lib/archive.html
92. http://librarystuff.net/
93. http://www.educationlibrarian.com/
94. http://www.libdex.com/weblogs.html
95. http://www.netlibrary.com/
96. http://www.clearinghouse.net/cgi-bin/chadmin/viewcat/Computers_and_Information_Technology/Internet_and_networking?kywd++
97. http://websearch.about.com/library/weekly/aa061903b.htm

98. http://websearch.about.com/cs/directories/tp/tpdirectories.htm

99. http://websearch.about.com/cs/metasearchengines/

100. http://websearch.about.com/library/weekly/aa061203a.htm

101. http://www.lib.duke.edu/libguide/evaluating_web.htm

102. http://www.library.cornell.edu/okuref/research/webcrit.html

103. http://www.lib.duke.edu/libguide/citing.htm#websites

CHAPTER 4

A Look At Search Engines

**"People forget how fast you did the job—
but they remember how well you did it."
-- Howard W. Newton**

An Overview:

We discussed several topics like searching techniques search engines, metasearch engines, directories, portals, vortals and invisible web in the previous chapter.

In this chapter, we plan to look at different search engines and shall learn about different search-portals (philosophies and methods) to find e-resources from the World Wide Web. However, due to limitations of scope of book, we can cover only major search engine sites. In this chapter, various features are taken directly from the respective web site of search provider, in order to make some analysis. The Internet contains a vast amount of information. Well, there are a lot of alternative search engines or portals. These types of Portals [which also provide search facility (to e-resources) in addition to other sort of resources] provide an entrance point for accessing the web. This means that they provide a variety of services and information. In some of the cases, the search engine is the foundation of the site and the other resources have been added to create a portal; on the other hand, other type of sites are basically portals and search facilities are included at later stage.

After completion of this chapter, you will be acquainted with several topics like identifying and locating (classifying) the resources available at the Internet, comparing one site with other similar sites, using the search features to search a particular site or topic, using directories to search a site, explaining the explored features to your friends and using some of the resources available at various sites.

Search engines are the best way of searching any information on any topic on our fingertips through Internet. According to StatMarket, Feb. 2002 "Search engines generate 7% to 8% of traffic to web sites." **After a Year,** StatMarket, Feb. 2003 says, "13 percent of traffic to web sites came from search engines, up from 8 percent the year before." They even help us in searching multimedia files and other deep web files as well. Many major search engines get their results by turning to third-party "**search providers**" to "power" their listings. To make matters more confusing, these search providers may run their own search engine sites, as well. Some of major search providers' names include Google, Inktomi, Overture, Open Directory, LookSmart, Teoma. Our discussion in this chapter is focused on and limited to some selected search engines irrespective of whether they are search providers or search users.

A brief comparison of size of textual documents (in billions) As of Sept 2, 2003

Error! Unknown switch argument.

KEY: GG=Google, ATW=AllTheWeb, INK=Inktomi, TMA=Teoma, AV=AltaVista.

Source: www.searchenginewatch.com

Fig. 4.1

Especially when there are several search engines available, a saying by Charles Dickens fits right "*No one is useless in this world that lightens the burden of another*". There are several types can be observed for search engines such as 'Free text search engines' or Index/Directory based search engines, Meta/Multi search engines, Natural language search engines. It's often quite difficult to define exactly what category a search engine should go into, because many of them now use a mix of the methods to find results. However, you can select one or two search engines as your preferred one. Fig. 4.2 depicts the working of search engines in a nice way. Once we know the working of search engines, we can jump on comparing one search engine to another by analysing the results we get for our desired queries. We take various search provider's site one by one for our study looking first at AltaVista.

Error! Unknown switch argument.

Fig. 4.2

(Source: http://www.searchtools.com/guide/index.html)

AltaVista

AltaVista has been viewed as the oldest search engine, and still considered a leading web search engine. It is backed by a rich history of innovations. Inventions include the first-ever multi-lingual search capability on the Internet. Like other web search engines, Altavista also provides Search toolbar to be installed at user's machine (to work with browser). Some key features are-

- Delivers Internet's first Web index (In Year1995)
- First multilingual search capabilities on the Internet.

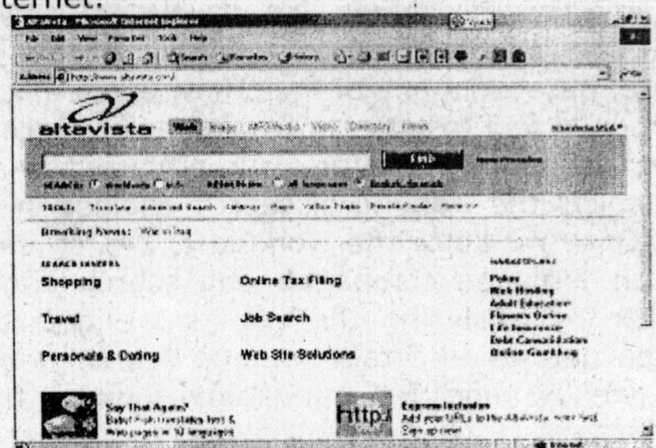

Fig. 4.3 (www.altavista.com)

- First Internet search engine to launch **Image, Audio, and Video search** capabilities

- Most advanced Internet search features and capabilities: multimedia search, translation & language recognition, and specialty search.
- Till date, awarded **61 search-related patents**, which is more than any other Internet search company.
- They launched "Babel Fish", the Web's first Internet machine translation service that can translate words, phrases or entire Web sites to and from English, Spanish, French, German, Portuguese, Italian and Russian etc.

SEARCH TIPS:

- To search for an **exact** phrase, put it in quotes (*Example:* "*what you want to see or not to see*").
- When you type multiple words in the search box, AltaVista looks for Web pages that contain all of the words. Uppercase and lowercase are treated the same. To maintain a certain capitalisation, put the word in quotes.
- Enter words that you think will appear on the Web page you want. AltaVista indexes all of the words on each Web page.
- Allow a user to instantly search in different areas: Web, Images, Audio, Video, Directory or News. Also searches in PDF Files.

Searching with AllTheWeb

AllTheWeb has emerged as a very popular search engine in recent years and has a capability of searching in different areas such as Web, News, Pictures, Video, Audio, FTP Files.

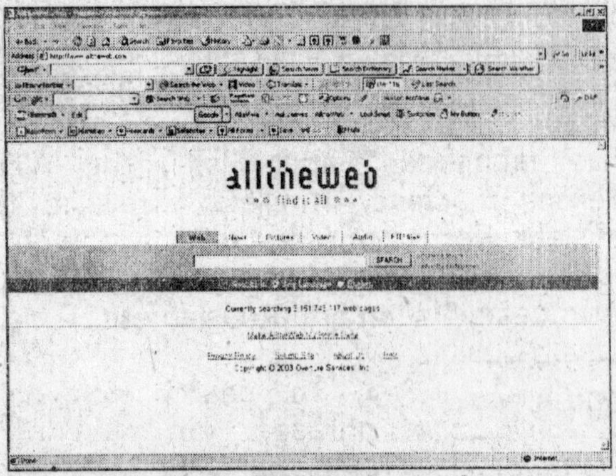

Fig. 4.4 (www.alltheweb.com)

According to its web site, the search engine is capable of searching in **3,151, 743,117** web pages. By using Advance feature, you can specify the parameters such as domains, various media files, file formats, even file size and date of updating.

It can also seach inside MS word and PDF Files. AlltheWeb supports searching in 49 different languages. It can provide latest news against news searches. AlltheWeb is a business of Overture Services Inc.(Overture.com) and claims to scan entire web in 7-11 days in order to provide fresh data agains a query submitted by a user.

Searching with Google

Google is also very popular search engine of today; it has complex, automated methods and an efficient search algorithm and thousands of low cost PC's networked together to create a very fast crawler-based search engine. It's website claims that it can search into **3,307,998,701** web pages.

The heart of google software is PageRank™, a system for ranking web pages developed by their founders Larry Page and Sergey Brin at Stanford University.

There are different categories to search such as Web, Images, Groups, Directory, and News.

Here, one feature is felt missing: - Audio- Video – MP3 Files Search facility (provided by AltaVista) is missing to some extent. There are many mirror sites maintained in different countries by Google. Indian mirror is available at www.google.co.in for requests coming from Indian ISP.

There are many languages in which you can see and use the Interface of the site.

Language translations are another very useful feature of the site. A remarkable feature of Google is the capability of searching within the PPT, PDF, DOC, XLS and other proprietary formats.

Many portals such as Go Networks (www.go.com), Indiatimes (www.indiatimes.com) use the google search facilities.

SEARCH TIPS: The Google Web Directory (directory.google.com) is a good place to start if you're not exactly sure which search keywords to use.

Google web site provides an example to explain directory features as, "searching for [Saturn] within the Science > Astronomy category of the Google Web Directory returns only pages about the planet Saturn, while searching for [Saturn] within the Automotive category returns only pages about Saturn cars. Searching within a category of interest allows you to quickly narrow in on only the most relevant pages to you."

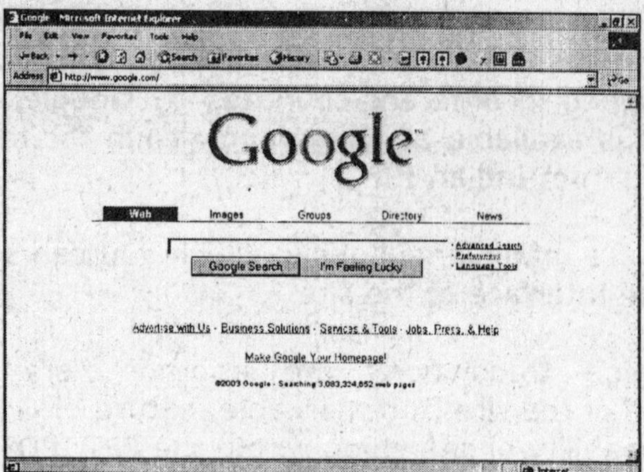

Fig. 4.5 (www.google.co.in)

SEARCH TIPS: By default, Google only returns pages that include all of your search terms. There is no need to include "and" between terms. As a rule, simple words such as who, what, where will not be considered for searching.

Still, If a common word is essential for you, you can include it by putting a "+" sign in front of it.

OR

By conducting a phrase search, which simply means putting quotation marks around two or more words. Common words in a phrase search (e.g., "what do you do") are included in the query formulation & thus will be searched.

A researcher can exclude a word from search by putting a minus sign ("-") immediately in front of the term he want to avoid.

If a researcher wants to search not only for a particular keyword, but also for its synonyms then you can place the tilde sign ("~") immediately in front of the keyword.

If a user wants to search within a known website but don't surely knows where the information is located within that site, he or she can enter keywords followed by the word "site" and a colon followed by the domain name. This is Domain Restriction feature of Google.

For example: To find President information on NIC site, one can enter:

President Site:www.nic.in and press search button, relevant pages from NIC Web Site will be displayed as results.

Google provides Search toolbar for IE and also browser buttons to add into browser's personal toolbar. Google also provides Web API's for software developers to automatically query Google. There are many other services like special searches, language translation, news search, image search, university search etc., which a user can take benefit of.

Yahoo

Yahoo is a very popular *portal site* containing around 25 mirror sites in different countries. Yahoo Groups are especially popular among many Indians, recently banned for Indian ISP due to the reason of propaganda against the state. [However, every site is available using in as prefix eg. www.in.groups.yahoo.com.] Yahoo Messenger service, Chat are other popular elements of this portal site.

Launched in 1994, Yahoo has been respected as the oldest "directory". Yahoo is still doing hard work to be a trafficked portal. The sequence of events shows this.

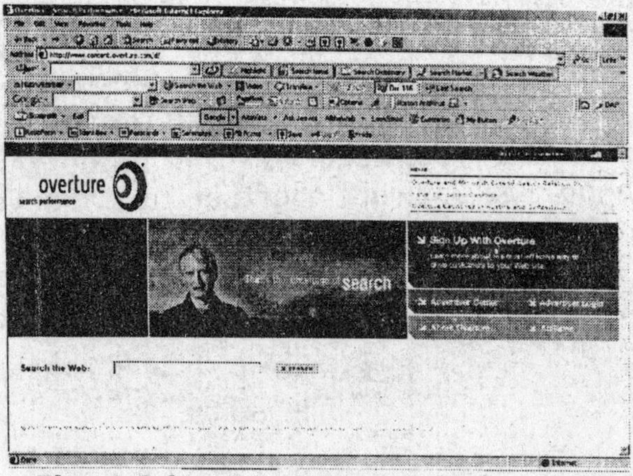

Fig. 4.6 (www.overture.com)

Earlier Yahoo used Google's services for its main results, but recently has discontinued this to produce main results. As of now, Yahoo has acquired the ***Inktomi*** *(www.inktomi.com)*, a leading search technology company known as provider of OEM Web Search, and many Internet Search destinations and content publishers depend upon Inktomi. ***Web Search 9***, is latest output of Inktomi and meets all other search engines in the key metrics of search performance: relevance, freshness and index size. Yahoo has also acquired ***Overture*** (www.overture.com) search technology.

All these developments are due to the desire of Yahoo to remain the most trafficked Internet destination worldwide. Let's switch again to Yahoo's searching features. Yahoo Network contains Yahoo Search as well as Yahoo Directory. Yahoo **Search** returns a list of web pages containing the words you entered. These results are a combination of sites from the entire Web (through a third-party search engine providers) and from the Yahoo Directory, While Yahoo **Directory** is a human-created and maintained library of web sites organized into categories and subcategories. The Yahoo Directory and Yahoo Search work together to bring you the information and resources you are looking for.

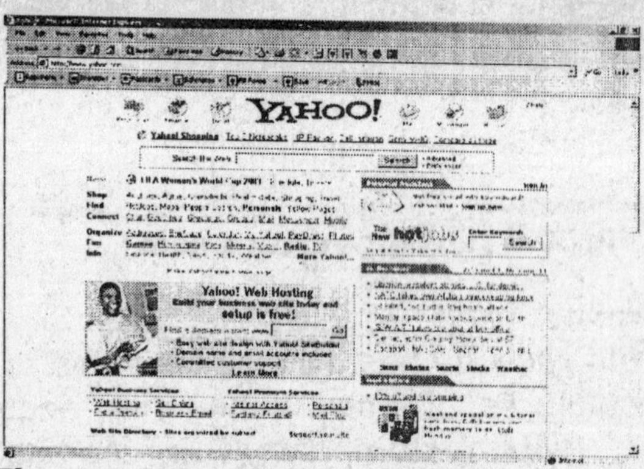

Fig. 4.7 (www.yahoo.com)

SEARCH TIPS:

Search for the words in exactly the order you enter them. This is similar to putting quotes (" ") around a set of words. Example: You're looking for a famous saying or quote: "I have a dream."

Different Searches available on yahoo (search.yahoo.com) are as listed below:

- Directory
- News
- Yellow Pages
- Images
- Cached

By searching into Cached you can get a copy of the page cached (saved) by the search engine, in case the site is unavailable.

In addition, one can now use personalisation feature of yahoo searches and save one's personal settings so they will apply every time.

By using Advanced Web Search you can search your specific criteria, including combinations of words and the date the site was last updated. Each type of search such as Web, Directory, or News, has its own Advanced Search page offering a unique set of options.

Yahoo also provides a search toolbar for integration with browsers. Another Important thing to note that is we can add the Yahoo! Search box to our web site, and very easy to set up. It's free too. One has to simply cut HTML code given by yahoo and paste into one's web site's HTML.

Excite

Excite (www.excite.com) is a portal and it also provides **metasearch** facility. By using Excite, you are searching these leading Web search engines: Google, Looksmart, Inktomi, Ask Jeeves, About, Overture, FindWhat etc.

Fig. 4.7 (www.excite.com)

There are searches available for Web, Directory, News, and Photos. As a simple experiment 'Try to search your name' by typing in the search text box and press search button, see the results compiled from different web search engines. Meta-search technology of Excite gives users the ability to search through all of these sites at the same time. In addition, personalisation of the site is also an available feature.

The **Excite Directory** also exists and in fact, it is a good compilation of Web sites, sorted subject-wise and reviewed by editors with expertise in their respective areas to ensure that the sorted order of web sites makes a sense, and increases the chance of quickly findings of exact results. E-mail, chat, boards and speedbar are other features available from the site.

SEARCH TIPS:

By inserting "AND" between words or the symbol "+" before a word, you can ask a specific combination of words be present in all search results.

MSN

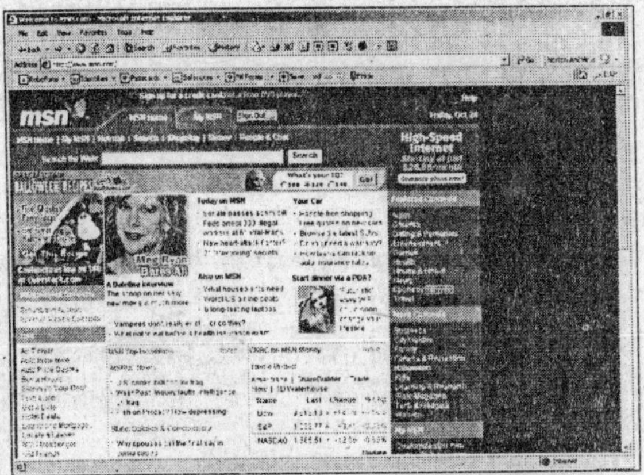

Fig. 4.8 (www.msn.com)

This Microsoft site is a very famous network portal (especially MSN Messenger) and also provides search facilities; sometime it shows a few differences from other search engines mentioned earlier. In addition to providing web directory, MSN Messenger, Chat room, job search, and music search are popular additional features. Especially **Encarta Encyclopedia (Encarta.msn.com)** is a very good, recommendable and huge archive for any learner to find out information from dictionaries, maps, guides and encyclopedia etc.

SEARCH TIPS:

MSN permits to use wildcards to find a related topic. For instance,

type Ind* to find pages containing Indo, India, Indian, and so on.

Lycos

One of the oldest search engines on the web, launched in 1994. Lycos network is a popular portal providing search, email, chat, messenger and other stuffs. Lycos Advanced Search is a precision tool that helps you get the most out of your Lycos Web search. The Advanced Search provides word filtering, URL and site name searching, and language querying.

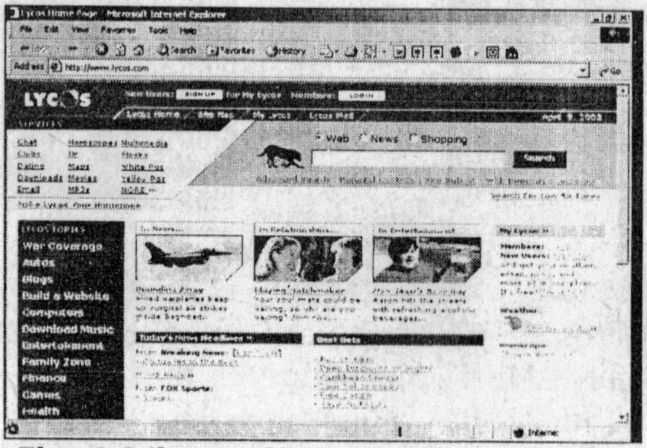

Fig. 4.9 (www.lycos.com)

The Advanced Search also allows you to retrieve web results within a variety of search catalogs such as Direct Hit, dMoz, and Overture. The site also provides *HotBot Quick Search Deskbar* as free download that can search over 200 search sites, from one searchbox.

SEARCH TIPS: **Use the plus sign (+) before a "must-have" word that you want to include: example x + y. To search for an exact phrase, you can put quotation marks (" x y") around your search term.**

Ask Jeeves

Ask Jeeves provides search in Web, Pictures, Products, News, and also to kids and as claimed by its web site (www.ask.com) it is "a search engine that could read your mind, one that understands what you are thinking when you type in a query. What you've imagined is Natural Language Processing (NLP). When we chat with friends, we speak in casual, conversational tones. It should be the same thing when you're looking for information online. With NLP, Jeeves is able to understand the context of what you are asking, and he can thus to offer you answers and search suggestions in the same human terms in which we all communicate."

Ask Jeeves delivers its search technologies and services through its own Web sites at Ask Jeeves (Ask.com) and Teoma.com. The search site claims to provide "a guided experience that helps people find the best answers on the Web. By aggregating best of breed search technologies, Ask Jeeves delivers the most relevant answers to users' queries and keyword searches". In addition, it provides Ask Jeeves toolbar to download and get integrated with IE browser.

Fig. 4.10 (www.ask.com)

Teoma, [means 'expert' in Gaelic] is unique from any other search engine. According to its website, *"It is the only search technology that can organize and analyze the Web as it is structured - in subject-based communities, returning the most authoritative and relevant results on the Web. Teoma is the primary search technology powering Ask.com, Ask.co.uk and Teoma.com. In fact,* Teoma is a crawler-based search engine owned by Ask Jeeves.

DirectHit (Teoma)

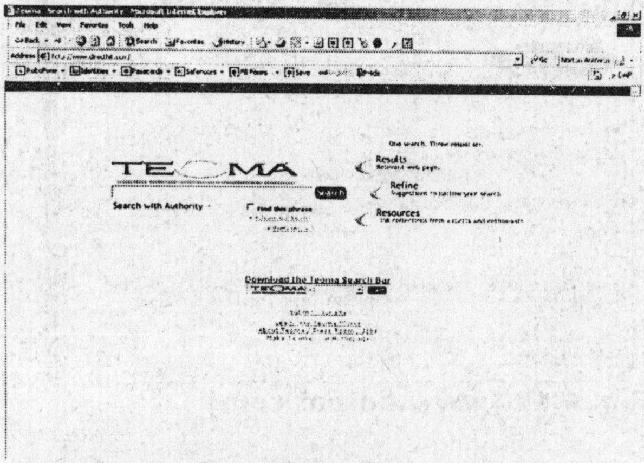

Fig. 4.11 (www.directhit.com)

The Directhit site interface is same as the Teoma search engine. In addition to utilising existing search techniques, Teoma applies authority, a new measure of relevance, to deliver authoritative search results.

To determine the level of authority associated with a particular site, Teoma employs three proprietary techniques: ***Refine, Results*** *and* ***Resources."*** Refine is basically suggestions to narrow your search to specific topics, while resources are listings made by Topic-experts. Directhit also offer to download Teoma Search Bar.

The Teoma Search Bar is **free** to download and if installed it appears every time you open a new Internet Explorer browser window.

HotBot

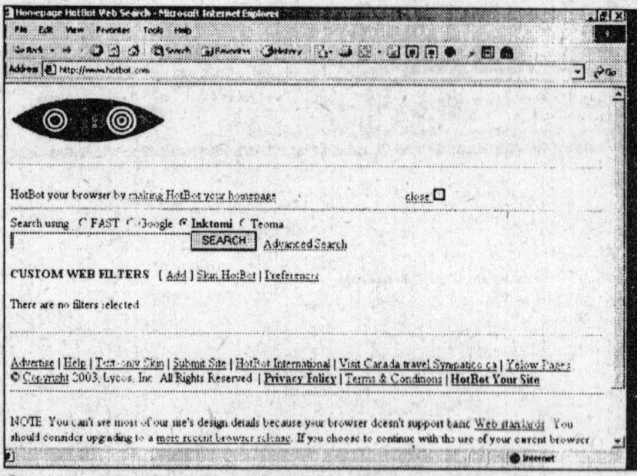

Fig. 4.12 (www.hotbot.com)

HotBot, is now a part of Lycos Network. It searches the full text of the more than 110 million documents in its database, finds all documents that fit your criteria, sorts them according to their relevance, and returns a list of documents in the form of abstracts and hyperlinks.

HotBot provides easy access to the web's four major sources: AllTheWeb.com, Google, Inktomi and Teoma, all of which are described earlier. Unlike a meta search engine, it cannot blend the results from all of these crawlers together. However, Hotbot also provides Search toolbar to be downloaded and integrated with IE browser.

Rediff

This Indian portal site provides search results, and sometime shows different from other search engines. It claims to search 1 billion web pages probably by employing some third party service. In addition, also provides email, chat, messenger, news and other stuffs.

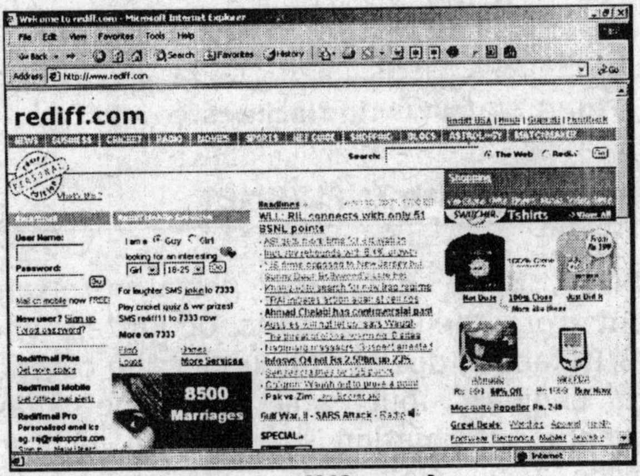

Fig. 4.13 (www.rediff.com)

Searching with Indiatimes

This Indian portal site provides search results, and sometime shows difference from other sites. This asks the user to search in Web or Indian sites or in Images. Presently employ a third party services (of *Altavista*) to produce the results. In addition, it also provides email, chat, messenger, news and other stuffs.

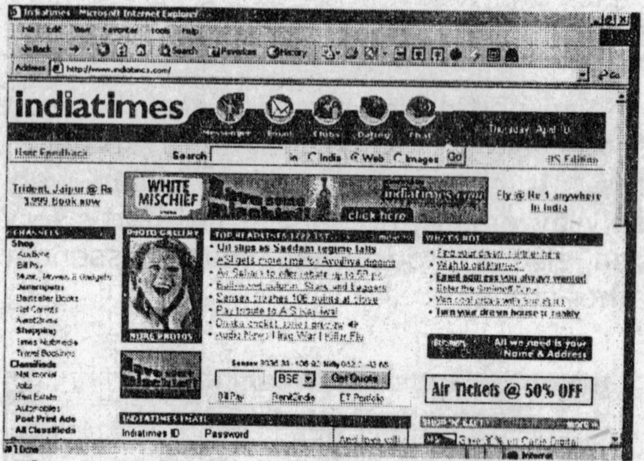

Fig. 4.14 (www.indiatimes.com)

Searching with INFLIBNET

INFLIBNET is a database portal (Vortal), and different from the other sorts of portals you seen before. In fact, it doesn't fall under the categories of search engines, but still someone may find bibliographic information search from its web site's databases.

From the index page, you should navigate to database section and then execute search for bibliographic details under any one of the databases e.g. books, serials, projects, thesis, experts etc. Browse yourself. NISSAT funded S & T database of experts may be prove useful to a researcher, who wishes to find an Indian expert.

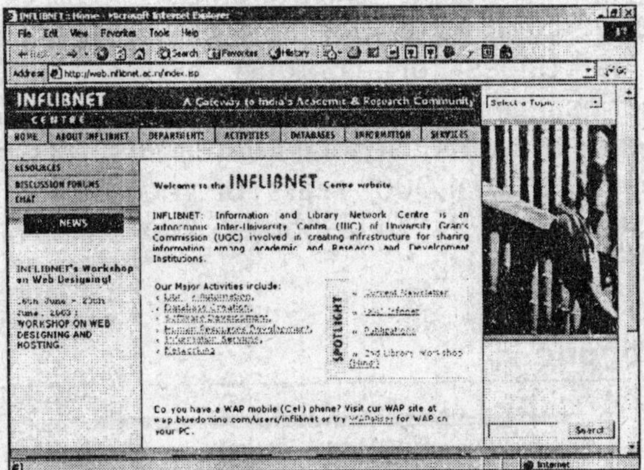

Fig. 4.15 (www.inflibnet.ac.in)

OCLC

Fig. 4.16 (www.oclc.org)

The OCLC web site contains bibliographic record and makes interests for librarians. WorldCat houses over 48 million bibliographic records. A typical record in WorldCat contains a physical description of an item and information about its intellectual content.

Through strategic partnerships, OCLC adds evaluative content to WorldCat bibliographic records such as tables of contents, cover art, book summaries, and notes about authors. WorldCat connects librarians, scholars, students, researchers and patrons to 4,000 years of recorded history—from stone tablets to e-books, wav recordings to MP3s.

Dogpile

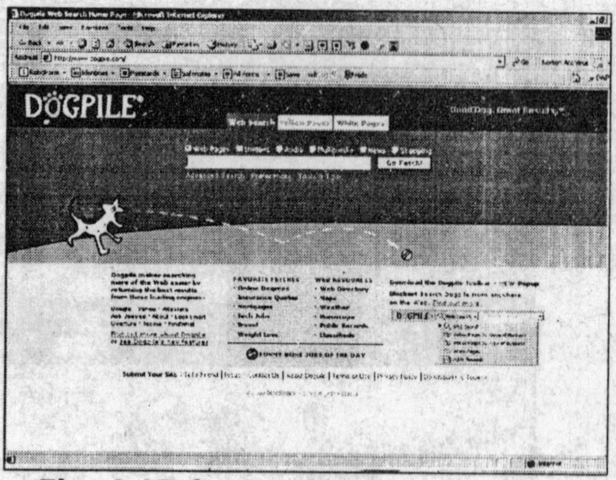

Fig. 4.17 (www.dogpile.com)

This is a good site to start with **metasearch** engines. **"Good Dog, Great Results"** is its trademark and claims the "Top Dog" of the search industry. Dogpile searches the Internet's top search engines such as Google, Yahoo, AltaVista, Ask Jeeves, About, FindWhat, LookSmart etc. Dogpile give you the options to search from Webpages, Images, Audio, Multimedia, News, Shopping. In addition offers Dogpile search toolbar to be downloaded and installed with IE Browser.

Profusion

Searching through Profusion **Metasearch** engine is really a nice experience. You can sign up with the site, and can create alerts and get alerts notification on your specific word from a web site (/page) on the event of add/modify of your desired word (/s). There are several vertical categories (groups), you can choose from which group to search from. Profusion submits your query to multiple search engines such as AOL, MSN, Teoma, Overture, Netscape, the entire web etc. and will produce results to you after retrieving the matches.

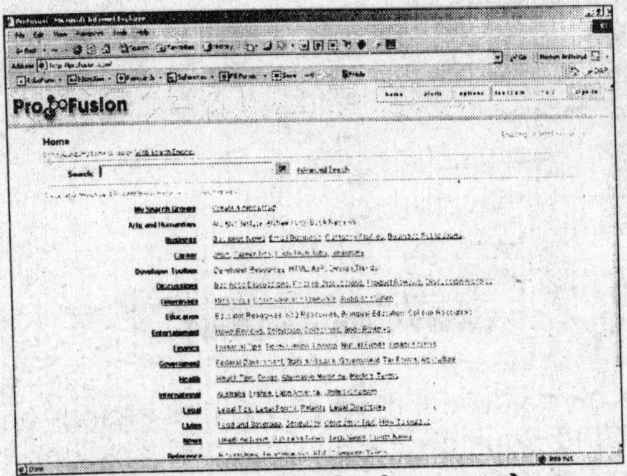

Fig. 4.18 (www.profusion.com)

Suppose you want to search for "sleep disorder" from Health Tips category, then you have to type

the text and click on the group /category you want to search. Great feature is that you can even create your own customized search groups – by easily organising search sources into groups that match your research needs. You have three choices namely- Fastest 5: / All: / You Choose: Out of them, you should select one.
Check yourself & Enjoy searching

In addition, you can also set all of the "Advanced" options for your groups, including number of results per source, search timeout, query type, and more.

Internet Sleuth

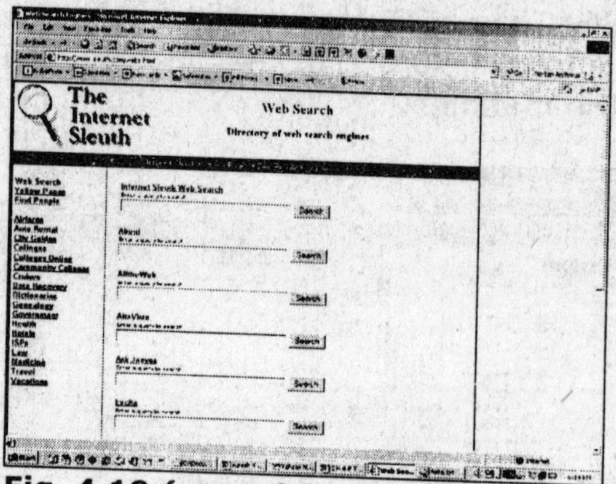

Fig. 4.19 (www.isleuth.com)

This site give you a listing of various search engines, you can find your query by typing in any one of text boxes and search.

It provides a collection of searchable sites, divided into several categories: Web search engines and directories, reviewed sites, news, business and finance, software etc.

By now, we have covered various popular portals in this chapter. The Internet, especially WWW is changing continuously. Where new sites and search engines emerge, at the same time some other is winding up its operations. Cautious users should identify the right search provider for their area & for their usage. Once you have grasped the art and science of searching the information resources from the sea of Internet, you will feel it easy. But as far as advanced readers are concerned, they might want to run their own Web Server and host web site, well supported by a digital collection. The rest of the book deals with advance topics in Part-II.

Useful URLs

(Used in this chapter and for further reading)

(All Accessed on Nov. 16, 2003)

1. 123India http://www.123india.com/
2. a2zIndia http://www.indiaconnect.com/a2zindia.htm
3. AltaVista India http://in.altavista.com/
4. Altavista Web site http://www.altavista.com
5. Appuonline http://www.appuonline.com/
6. Best Indian Sites http://www.bestindiansites.com/
7. BharathSeek http://www.bharathseek.com/
8. Cyberindian http://www.cyberindian.com/

9. Google Directory directory.google.com
10. E-Mews http://www.e-mews.com/e-india.htm
11. MSN Encarta encarta.msn.com
12. forindia http://www.forindia.com/
13. Goodhit India http://www.goodhit.com/
14. Google Web site http://www.google.com
15. http://searchenginewatch.com/reports/article.php/2156471
16. http://www.indiana.edu/~librcsd/search/meta.html
17. ZapMeta http://www.zapmeta.com/
18. Iloveindia http://www.iloveindia.com/
19. India Bridge http://www.theindiabridge.com/
20. India Engine http://www.indiaengine.com/
21. India Web Services http://www.indiawebservices.net/directory/
22. IndiaA2Z http://indiaa2z.com/
23. Indiaatlas http://www.indiaatlas.com/
24. IndiaConnect http://www.indiaconnect.com/
25. India's First Web Guide http://www.indianindex.com/
26. Indias.com http://www.indias.com/
27. IndoSeek http://www.indoseek.com/
28. Jadoo http://www.jadoo.com/
29. Khoj http://www.khoj.com/index.html
30. LinktoIndia http://www.linktoindia.com/
31. Lookaddress http://www.lookaddress.com/
32. Lycos Asia - India http://in.lycosasia.com/
33. Lycos Web site http://www.lycos.com
34. MSN India http://www.msn.co.in/

35. NewIndia http://www.newindia.com/seek/
36. Punjabi Network http://www.punjabi.net/
37. Search Engine Watch www.searchenginewatch.com
38. Search India http://www.searchindia.com/
39. SearchTools
    http://www.searchtools.com/guide/index.html
40. SouthIndia http://www.southindia.com/
41. SurfIndia http://www.surfindia.com/
42. WebIndia http://www.webindia.com/
43. AllTheWeb Web site www.alltheweb.com
44. Ask Web site www.ask.com
45. DirectHit Web site www.directhit.com
46. DogPile Web site www.dogpile.com
47. Excite Web site www.excite.com
48. Go Web site www.go.com
49. Google India Web site www.google.co.in
50. HotBot Web site www.hotbot.com
51. YahooGroups India Web site www.in.groups.yahoo.com
52. Indiatimes Web site www.indiatimes.com
53. INFLIBNET Web site www.inflibnet.ac.in
54. Inktomi Web site www.inktomi.com
55. ISleuth Web site www.isleuth.com
56. MSN Web site www.msn.com
57. NIC Web site www.nic.in
58. OCLC Web site www.oclc.org
59. Overture www.overture.com
60. Profusion Web site www.profusion.com

61. Rediff Web site www.rediff.com
62. Teoma Web site www.teoma.com
63. Yahoo Web site http://www.yahoo.com

CHAPTER 5

Setting up Web Servers for Library

"Pleasure in the job puts perfection in the work."
-- Aristotle

Web Server: An Overview

Every computer on the Internet is called Host. A host providing Web-contents is called Web Server. A simple analogy will tell that like people reside in their homes, similarly **web sites reside on web servers**. A Web server is software, which enable a computer machine to act as a server, which can fulfill request for information made by a browser running on a client computer on intranet or Internet.

Today, there are many web server software packages available. A web server has the capabilities to publish a web site, which is in turn a set of directories, sub directories, script files etc.

A web server is loaded on a server machine. Running instance of a web server software, manages a web sites; it accept requests from clients for web pages, retrieves appropriate page from hard disk and sends the page back to client, who had made requests. Some examples of the popular web server software are IIS, Apache, and

PWS. According to the *"June 2003 Netcraft web server survey"* made by NetCraft Company, (www.NetCraft.com) Apache is mostly used web server worldwide.

Name / Acronym	**Full Name**	**Supplier/ Company**	**Operating System**
PWS	*Personal Web Server*	*Microsoft*	*Win 95/98/2000*
IIS	*Internet Information Server*	*Microsoft*	*Win 2000/NT*
Apache	*Apache Web Server*	*Apache*	*Win 2000/ NT, Linux*
Netscape	*Netscape Web Server*	*Netscape*	*Win 2000/ NT, Linux*

Table 5.1 Various web server software

Abraham Lincoln had once said *"You cannot help men permanently by doing for them what they could and should do for themselves"*. This is a true and very relevant fact of life; we should attain self-reliance and confidence. Although the installation of web servers is more technical than installing word processing or paint program, but we must do ourselves the installations and configurations of web server software's in order to learn and to get technical skills. The rest of the text is intended to help or guide you by providing some steps and screenshots to do the installation & configuration of two popular web servers namely IIS and Apache.

Installation and configuration of Internet Information Services (IIS)

This is Microsoft's web server designed for the Windows NT platform.

Commonly known as IIS; is in fact a suite of services – WWW, FTP and Gopher. WWW is meant for World Wide Web publishing, FTP for File Transfer protocol. IIS is a Windows based web server software and can run on operating system such as Win NT or Windows 2000 and cannot run on non-windows operating system such as Linux or Unix. IIS is not meant to be used on Win 98 or Win XP as these operating systems are supposed to be used on the user-end and these Operating Systems not to be used as servers. IIS allows WWW, FTP and Gopher protocols on network. In fact, simply speaking IIS is a windows component that makes it easy to publish information and makes it easy for you to create a strong platform for network application. Key features include better ASP flow control and faster processing for scriptless ASP pages. The combination of Windows 2000 with IIS 5.0 makes it possible to create a full spectrum of Internet and Intranet sites that take advantage of the technologies you already have in place.

Installation of IIS

Since IIS can run on the Win NT or Win 2000 Operating Systems, it is presumed that Win 2000 is being used on your machine as well. For security purposes. 'Microsoft recommends that all drives planned to be with IIS should be formatted with NTFS file System'.

Please note that if you have upgraded to Win 2000, IIS 5.0 will be installed by default, only if PWS was installed on your previous version of windows operating system.

For administrators, it is easier to install and manage IIS. IIS 5.0 is installed as part of the Windows 2000 installation process. IIS 5.0 is not installed on Win 2000 professional by default, however, you can install it by selecting additional components by using the **Add/Remove Programs** application in the control panel.

Installation Steps:

1. Go to **Start >> Settings>> Control Panel** and then start the **Add/Remove Programs** application. Something similar to Figure 5.1 will appear on your monitor screen.

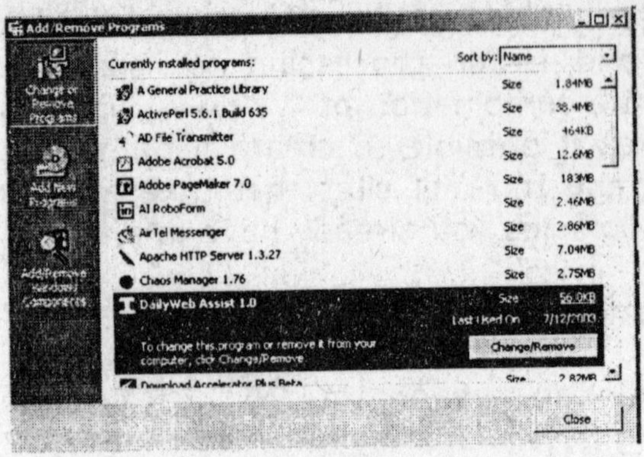

Fig. 5.1

2. Select **Add/Remove Windows Components** and then similar to Figure 5.2, will appear on your screen. Tick all the check boxes, and move the mouse so that the mouse pointer points at the next button in the dialog box and click once.

   The dialog box, then on the next screen, will prompt you to click on finish button. If you are having Windows 2000 Operating System, then you can even install version 6.0 of IIS by downloading from Microsoft site (www.microsoft .com). Latest versions are always available there.

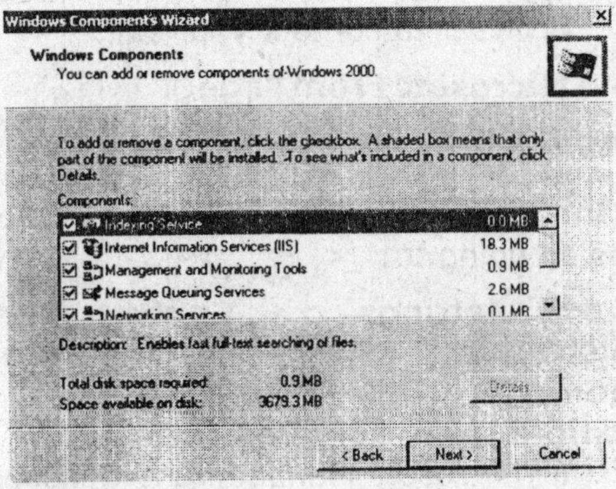

Fig. 5.2

Minimum requirements for IIS software:

Internet Information Services requires that the following software be installed on the computer prior to installation:

1. A Computer running Windows NT server 4.0, [with service pack 6] or **Windows 2000** or later.

2. A fully configured network, running **TCP/IP** Protocol. In all cases TCP/IP networking must be installed.

Additional optional components

- **The Domain Name System** (DNS) service installed on a computer in your intranet. Web sites usually use the Domain Name System. If you register a domain name for your site, users can type your site's domain name in a browser to contact your site.
- **Microsoft FrontPage.**

Running IIS Service

You can start Windows Internet Information Services by going to:

Start >> Settings >> **Control Panel >> Administrative Tools** >> **Computer Management** Then expand the **Server Applications and Services** node in the console tree of the Microsoft Management Console (MMC) by clicking on the **+** icon in the left, and select **Internet Information Services**, as shown in Figure below.

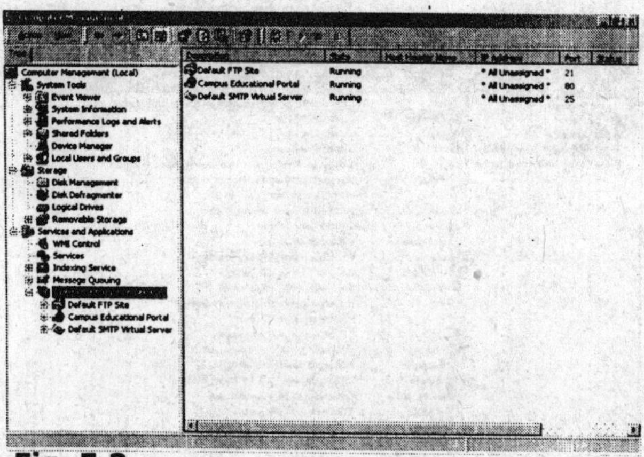

Fig. 5.3

Now, you will be able to see various component services of IIS, you can start, stop and restart any of the services, which are part of IIS by using the interface options. IIS 5.0 is managed using the Internet Information Services Microsoft Management Console (MMC) snap-in. Previously this tool was called Internet Service Manager (ISM). This administration tool for IIS 5.0 is integrated with other administrative functions of Windows 2000.

ISM / MMC

You can access this management tool by clicking **Start >> Settings >> Control Panel >> Administrative Tools**, then clicking on **Internet Services Manager**. This is a very popular interface utility to control and configure IIS and is preferred by most of the System Analysts and Webmasters due to the wide options available at a single place.

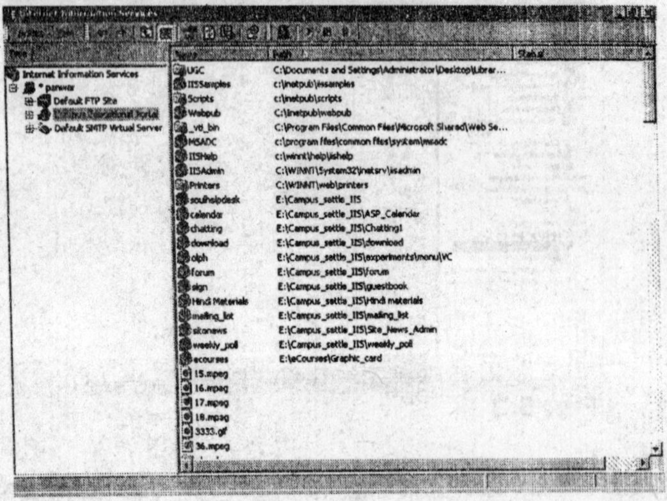

Fig. 5.4

Online Help Manual

Reading the online-help is the best practice in Computer Science. After installation, you can reach to online help documents, by typing **http://localhost/iisHelp/** in your browser address bar and then pressing ENTER. These are supplied along with IIS. You will find lots of help pages there, and they prove very useful while learning about IIS and its use.

Testing

-On the same machine

1. After installing, you can test your installation by using a browser either Netscape Navigator or Internet

Explorer Start a Web browser, such as Microsoft Internet Explorer.

2. Type in the Uniform Resource Locator (URL) for your new server or type http://localhost.

3. For example, if your computer network identification is given as suresh, then in the Address box you should type: http://suresh/ then press ENTER. The welcome page of IIS should appear on the screen.

-On your Intranet

4. Ensure that your computer has an active network connection and is available and visible from some other pc.

5. Repeat Step 1 and 2 described above.

> If a web site is accessible on the Intranet then, by registering that computer with the Domain Name Server (DNS), it can be made available on the Internet provided you have the Internet connectivity.

Managing IIS Services

IIS can be managed locally as well as remotely.

IIS can be managed locally by

- Microsoft management Console (MMC).
- Windows Services

and remotely by

- Web based Administration Tools/ HTMLA (for 6.0)
- MMC

If you want to administer an IIS Server remotely then MMC should be installed along with Windows 2000 on the remote client. In addition, Internet firewall protecting IIS Server should be configured in such a way that it shall allow the necessary communication.

IIS 5.0 has Web-based administration tools that allow remote management of a server from any browser. IIS 6.0 can be configured from the *remote administration (HTML) tool*. The browser-based Internet Services Manager (HTMLA) lets you remotely administer certain IIS features over the Internet, if you logon by using administrator password.

Publishing Information

By default, your WWW service will look at **C:\inetpub\www** for HTML content to be published. The initial default document (that IIS looks for when entering a directory) is **default.htm**. This can be changed using the **Internet Service Manager**, which is really a very much helpful Graphical User Interface. You can, however, change the default directory and the default document (inside that directory) by using Internet Service Manager. Once you have done that, IIS will show your preferred document, when someone visits your site.

Steps: -

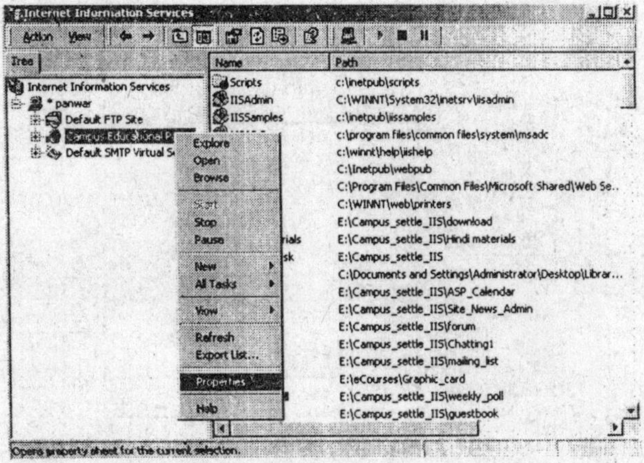

Fig. 5.5

1. **Open ISM** by clicking **Start >> Settings >> Control Panel >> Administrative Tools**, then clicking on **Internet Services Manager**
2. Right click on the Website, you want to

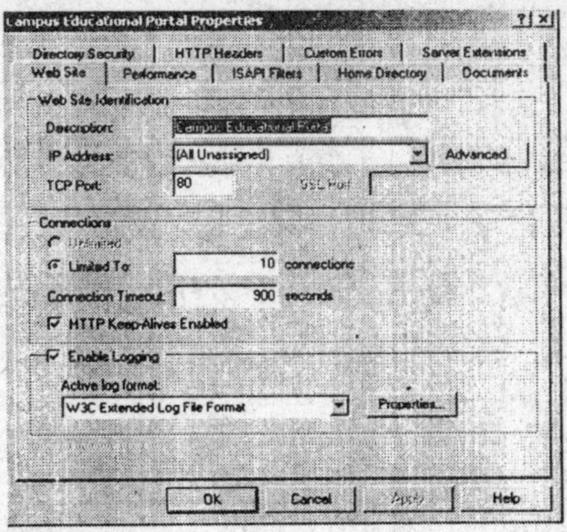

Fig. 5.6

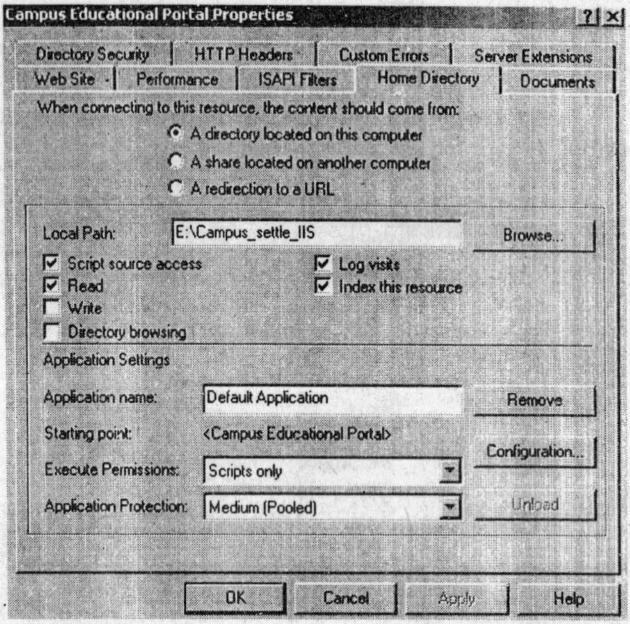

Fig. 5.7

configure for publishing your information. Click on the **Properties** in popup menu.

3. Click the **Home Directory** tab, and then specify where your home directory is located. You can select one of these:
    - **A directory** located on a hard disk on your computer. [Fig 5.7]
    - A shared directory located on another computer.
    - A redirection to a URL.

In the text box, specify the path name, share name, or URL of your directory. In Fig 5.7, it becomes clear that we have mentioned

\campus_settle_IIS directory in E drive as our home directory.

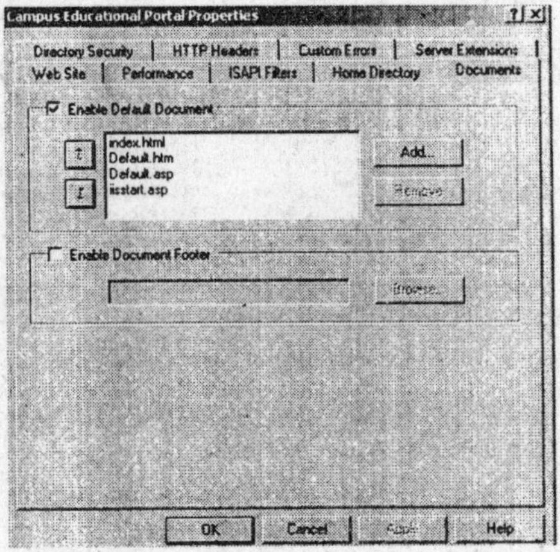

Fig. 5.8

4. If you select first option, then you have to specify which document you want to show as first page (Home Page of your site). In Fig 5.8, we have given Index.html as Home Page of our site.

5. Press Ok

6. Right Click on the Website and click on Browse (as shown in Fig. 5.9).

7. If you are able to see your web site, then you are successful.

Delegated Administration for distribution of workload

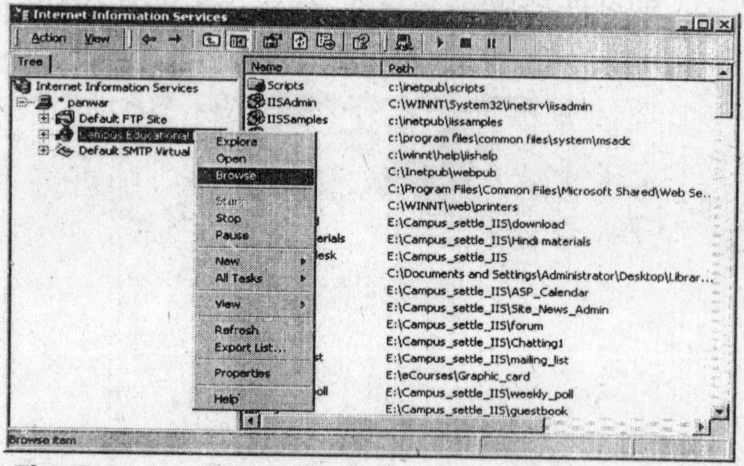

Fig. 5.9

This is a useful feature to ISPs or someone who wishes to use only one webserver to host more then one web site. Imagine, an ISP that hosts sites for a number of different companies, can assign delegates from each company as the Operators for each individual company's Web site. Operators can administer properties that affect only their respective sites. They do not have access to properties that affect other companies' sites, global parameters of IIS, the server computer or the network. IIS allows administrators to set up administration accounts called *Web Site Operators* with limited administration privileges on Web sites. This lets an ISP administrator who hosts multiple Web sites on a single server delegate the day-to-day management of the Web site to their respective company's IT department without giving up total administrative control.

Unix/Linux based web servers

Many free web servers for non-windows platform are available for free download. For these web servers, they have **a configuration file**, which is the most important, and that file has detailed documentation of various options. By reading comments inside the file, you can configure and reconfigure these servers; the file is **httpd.conf** (httpd: Hypertext transfer protocol daemon). After configuring the server by editing the file, the server is ready to be started. In order to start and stop the 'http daemon' (httpd) you should have root access. As you already know that, the most commonly used web servers for such Operating System is Apache. It is available for free download from the site: http://www.apache.org. **The Apache web server can also be used on Windows Operating System without any problem.** The Apache web server shall be used to host a Digital Library System, which we will be learning and developing in the last Chapter of this book, by doing hands-on experiments. In the remaining part of this chapter, our focus will be on Apache Web Server under Windows Environment.

Installation and Configuration of Apache (For Windows)

According to Apache website, **"Apache on NT has not yet been optimized for performance.** Apache still performs best, and is most reliable on Unix platforms. Over time NT performance has improved, and great progress is being made in the upcoming version 2.0 of Apache for the Windows platforms."

We will learn how to install, configure and run Apache 1.3 under Microsoft Windows operating system in this chapter. And later, in chapter 7 we will use Greenstone Software on the top of Apache 1.3 to build a digital library.

Downloading Apache

You may find the latest version available for download at the Apache web site, at http://www.apache.org/dist/httpd/, You may download the binary build of Apache for Windows named as `apache_1_3_#-win32-no_src.msi` file for our experiments.

Minimum requirements for Apache software:

The following software be installed on the computer prior to installation:

1. A Computer running Windows NT server 4.0 (with service pack 6) or **windows 2000** or later.
2. 2. A fully configured network, running TCP/IP Protocol. In all cases **TCP/IP** networking must be installed.

Note1 and Note 2 mentioned by Apache online help manual are worth a look:

"***Note 1:*** *Apache 1.3 is designed to run on Windows NT 4.0 and Windows 2000. The binary installer will only work with the x86 family of processors, such as Intel's. Apache may also run* *on Windows 95 and 98, but these have not been tested."*

"Note: 2 "Winsock2" is required for Apache 1.3.7 and later. *Windows 2000 have already have Winsock2 components, so Windows 2000 and NT (Service Pack 3 or later) users need not to worry. "*

Additional optional components

- **Microsoft Installer version 1.10** must be installed on your PC before you can install the Apache. (Windows 2000 and Windows ME are both delivered with the Microsoft Installer support; others will need to download it.)
- **The Domain Name System** (DNS) service installed on a computer in your intranet
- **Microsoft FrontPage**

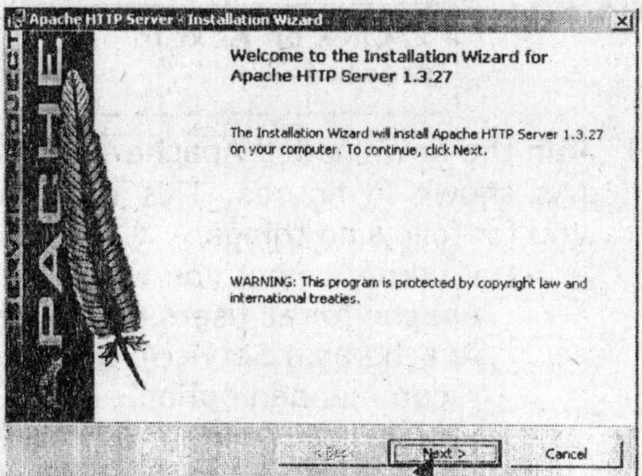

Fig. 5.10

Click here to proceed

Installation Steps

Please make note of the following things before you start installation.

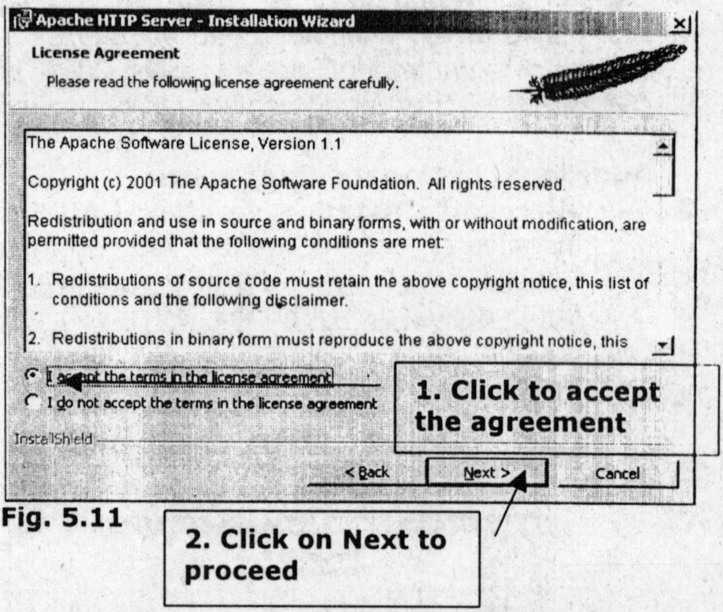

Fig. 5.11

1. Run the downloaded Apache `.msi` file. (As shown in figures. This will ask from you for following things:
    - Whether or not you want to run Apache for all users (installing Apache as a Service), a recommended option.
    - Your Server name, Domain name and administrative email account.)
2. You may follow the on-screen installations to finish the installation

process. The Figures from 5.10 to 5.19 shown below explains each and every step towards the completion of the process. The other things to be noted are written below.

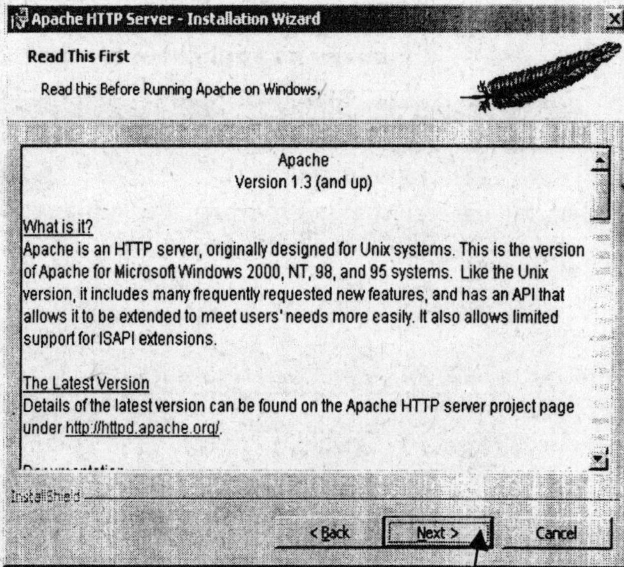

Fig 5.12

Click on Next to proceed

3. During the installation, Apache will configure the files in the `conf` directory. However if you are installing apache second time, or later, any of the files in this directory already exist they will **not** be overwritten. If you eventually uninstall Apache, your configuration and log files will not be removed. You will need to

delete the installation directory tree ("C:\Program Files\Apache Group" by default) yourself. For more information, check with the online help manual.

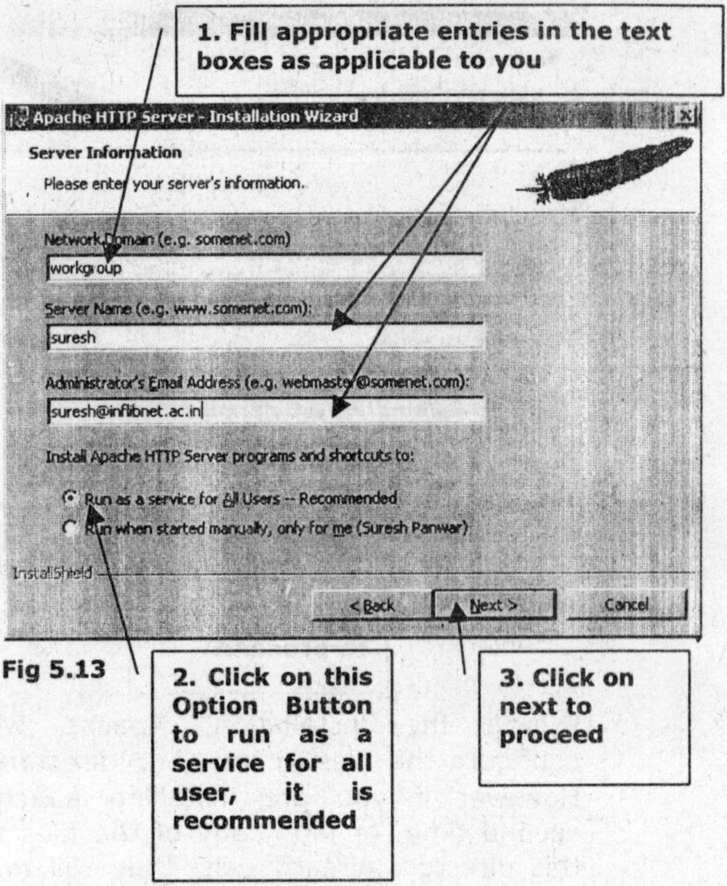

Fig 5.13

4. This would mean it is safe to install Apache over an existing installation (but you will have to stop the existing server

running before doing the installation, then start the new one after the installation is finished).

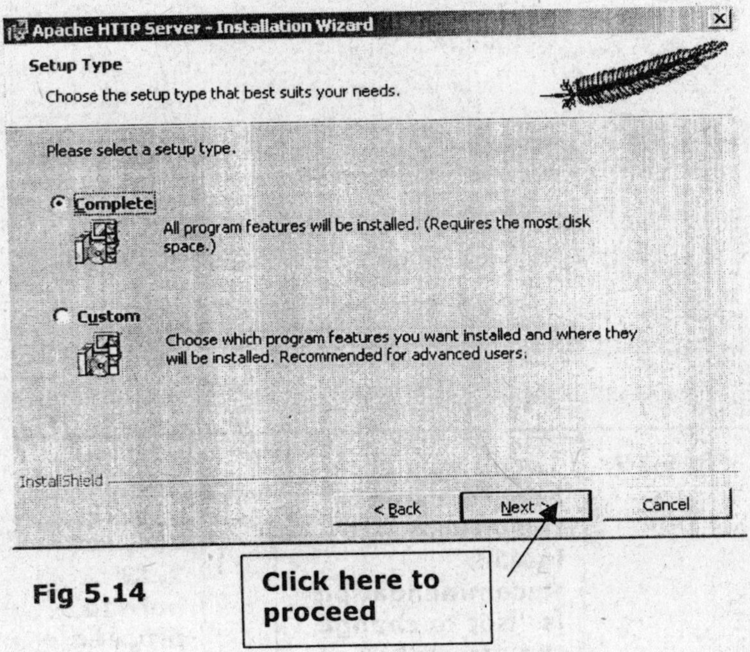

Fig 5.14

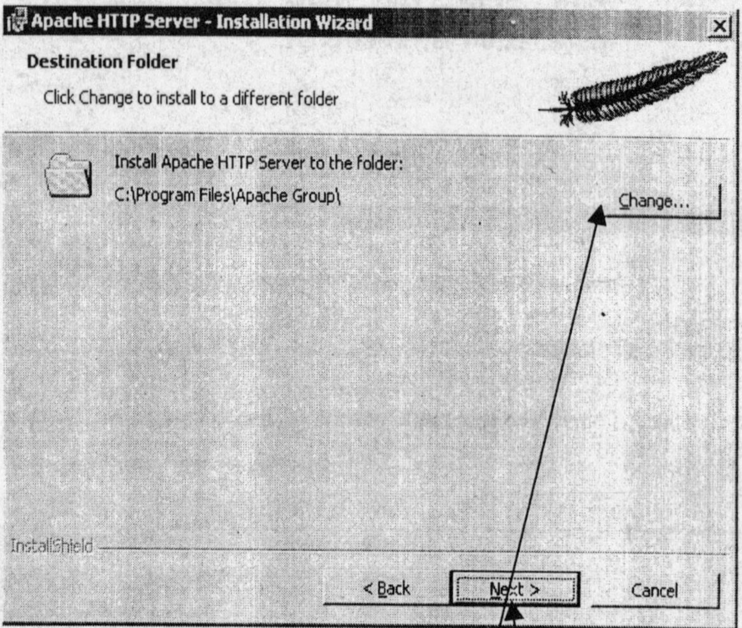

Fig 5.15

1. You may click here to change the directory to install. Recommendation is "Not to change the directory " at first installation

2. Click here to proceed

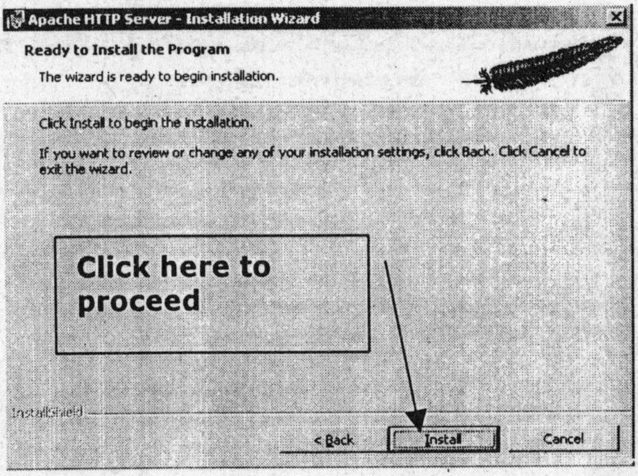

Fig 5.17

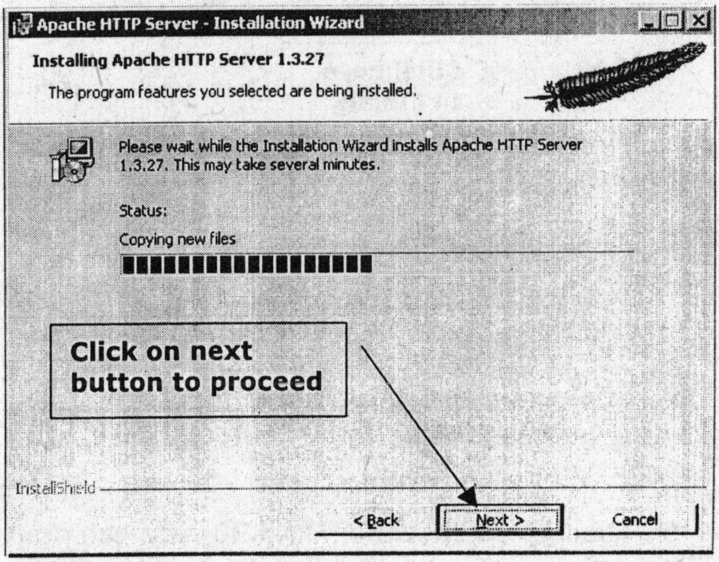

Fig 5.18

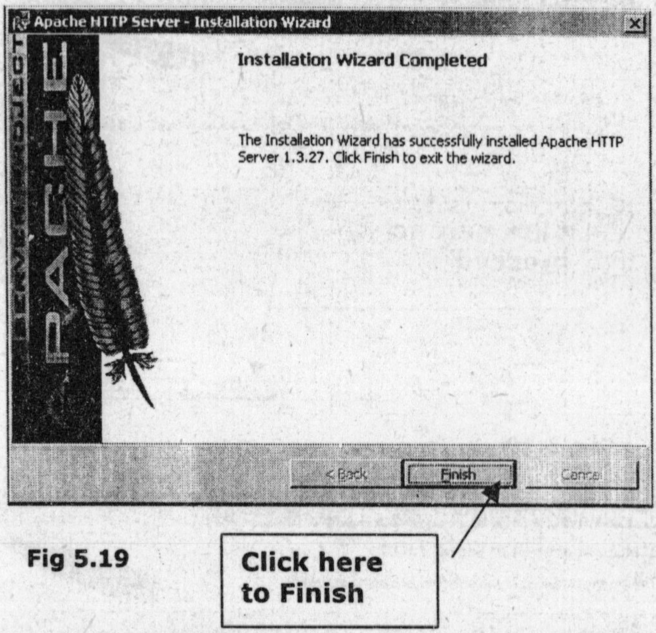

Fig 5.19

Running Apache

There are two ways you can run Apache:

1. As a "service".
2. From a console window. Closing this console window will terminate the Apache server.

In the above installation, (see Fig 5.13) we have chosen choice number 1 as this is the best option; because we want Apache to automatically start when your machine boots.

To run Apache, as shown in Fig 5.20, you can start HTTP server by going **Start>>programs>> Apache HTTP Server>>Control HTTP Server** and then click on **start**. The next screen, similar to 5.21 will appear on the screen and inform that the server has been started.

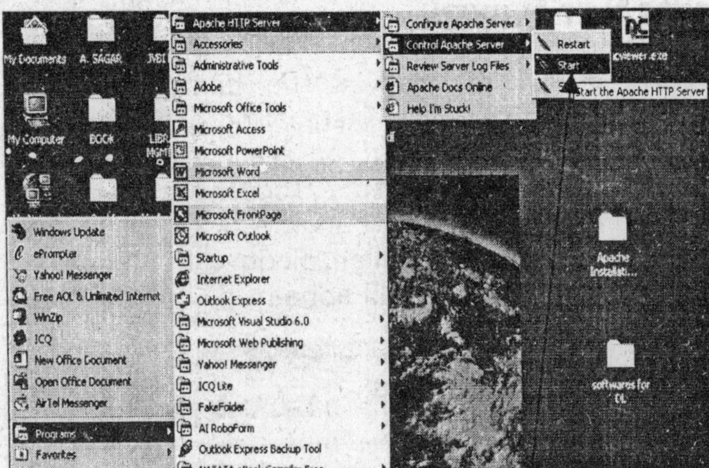

Fig 5.20

Click here to start the Apache Web Server

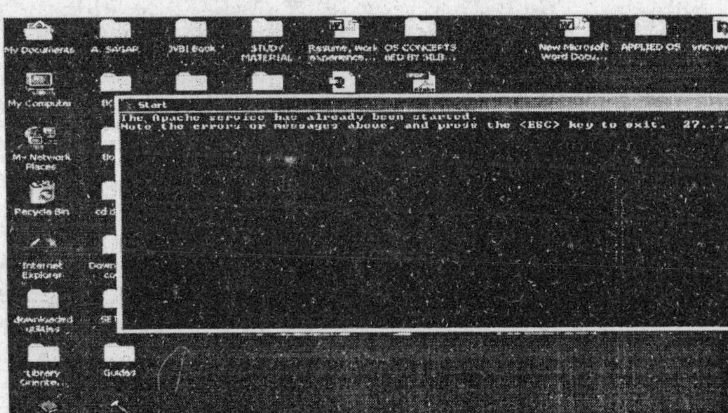

Fig 5.21

Online Help Manual

Reading the online-help is the best Practice in Computer Science. After Installation of Apache (on port 80 -By default), you can reach to online help documents, by typing **http://localhost/manual/** in your browser address bar and pressing ENTER. These manuals are supplied along with Apache. A window similar to 5.22 will appear.

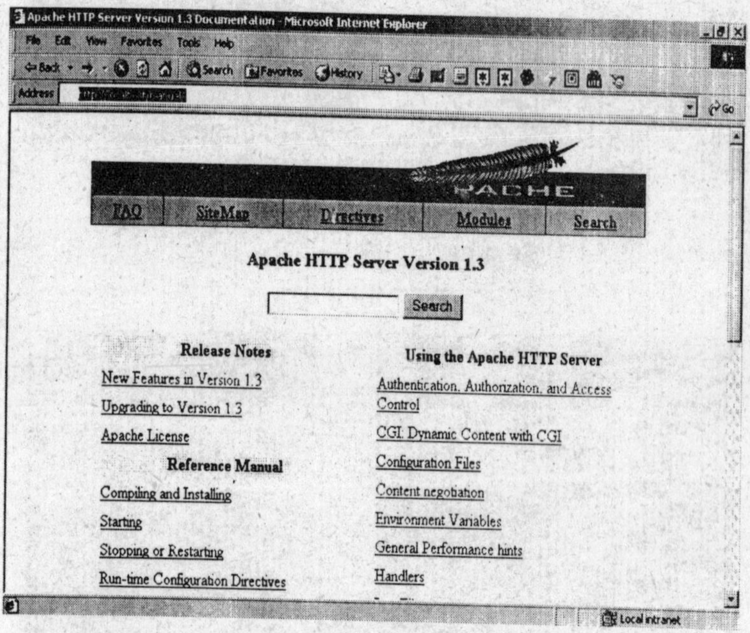

Fig 5.22

Testing

-On the same machine

After starting Apache running (either in a console window or as a service) it will listen to port 80 (unless you changed the `Port`, `Listen` or `BindAddress` directives in the configuration files). Test your apache installation by typing http://localhost/ in browser. This should respond with a welcome page, and a link to the Apache manual. If nothing happens or you get an error, you will be required to look in the `error.log` file in the `logs` directory.

Once your basic installation is working, you should configure it properly by editing the files in the `conf` directory.

1. After installing, you can test your installation by using address of your machine in the browser. Start a Web browser, such as Microsoft Internet Explorer.

2. Type in the Uniform Resource Locator (URL) for the home directory of your new server.

-on your Intranet

3. Ensure that your computer has an active network connection and that the DNS server service (or other name resolution method) is functioning.

4. Repeat Step 1 and 2 described above from some other computer on the network.

Configuring Apache Services for Windows

Files in the conf directory configure Apache. There are a few different directives for Apache on Windows. Begin configuring the Apache server by reviewing httpd.conf and its directives. File httpd.conf contains a great deal of documentation itself, followed by the default configuration directives recommended when starting with the Apache server. Begin by reading these comments to understand the configuration file, and make small changes.

The main differences in Apache for Windows are:

- Because Apache for Windows is multithreaded; So, "process"-management directives are different:
    - MaxRequestsPerChild - The recommended default is `MaxRequestsPerChild 0`.
    - ThreadsPerChild - The recommended default is `ThreadsPerChild 50`.
- Because Apache uses Unix-style names internally, you must use forward slashes, not backslashes.
    - For example *c:/abc/xyz.html* is written correctly.
- Apache can also load ISAPI Extensions such as those used by Microsoft's IIS, and other Windows servers. But note that Apache *CANNOT* load ISAPI Filters.

Publishing Information

By default, Apache WWW service will look at DocumentRoot: the directory out of which you will serve your documents. By default, all requests are taken from DocumentRoot "C:/Program Files/ Apache Group/Apache/htdocs/ and the default file content to be published is index.html.en. You can, however, change the default directory and the default document inside that directory.

Document Root

This is an important directive which sets the directory from which httpd will serve files. It is written in httpd.conf file, which is a configuration file for HTTP Daemon. You can change value of DocumentRoot by mentioning some other directory or subdirectory. An Example is shown below:

```
DocumentRoot /suresh/web
```

Running IIS and Apache concurrently on a PC

Many people may find themselves reluctant in accepting that two web servers can run on a pc; but it is possible. In this part, we will learn how to run two web servers Apache and IIS on a single machine. Because, two Web Server *CANNOT* share the same TCP/IP port with each other and thus logic say that two web servers cannot run concurrently at a time, you may need to stop or uninstall one of them.

You can run both servers concurrently by applying a trick of changing the port these two applications are listening two. By default, both of these two will listen to port number 80, unless you change the configurations. The trick is to change the port of any one of the web server service. Reconfigure either Apache or the IIS so that they do not listen on the same TCP/IP port. You may find the Windows "netstat -an" command useful in finding out what ports are in use. You can change configuration of either IIS or Apache as per your wish. Here both the methods are provided for the readers help.

Changing port of IIS

1. **Open ISM** by clicking **Start >> Settings >> Control Panel >> Administrative Tools**, then clicking on **Internet Services Manager**

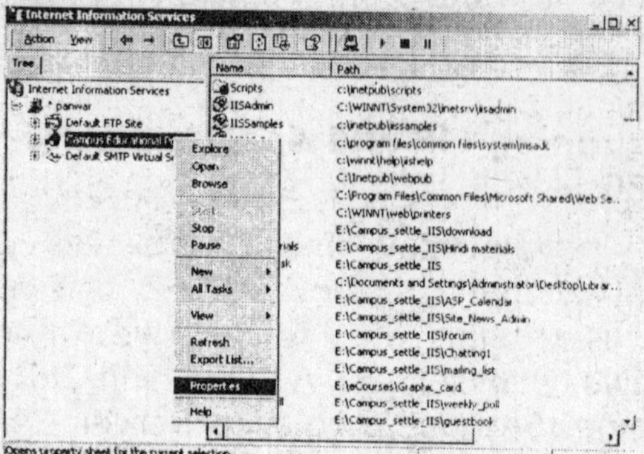

Fig 5.23

2. Right click on the Website, you want to configure for publishing your information. Click on the **Properties** in popup menu.

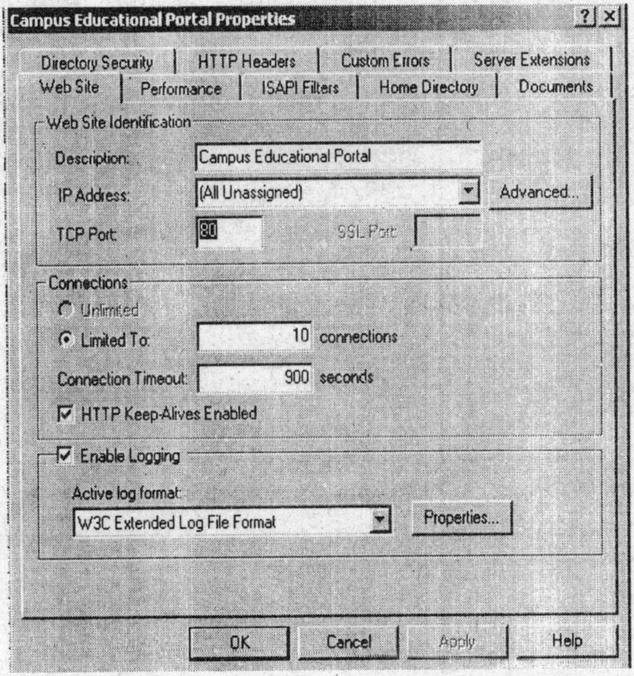

Fig 5.24

3. Write in the focused textbox (as shown in Fig 5.24), the alternative TCP/IP port, which you wish to use, for example say 800, then press ok

4. Test by typing in the browser http://localhost:80 (or in this example http://suresh:800/)

Changing port of Apache

1. **Open httpd** by clicking **Start >> Programs** >> **Apache HTTP Server >> Configure Apache Server**, then clicking on **Edit the HTTPD.conf Configuration File**

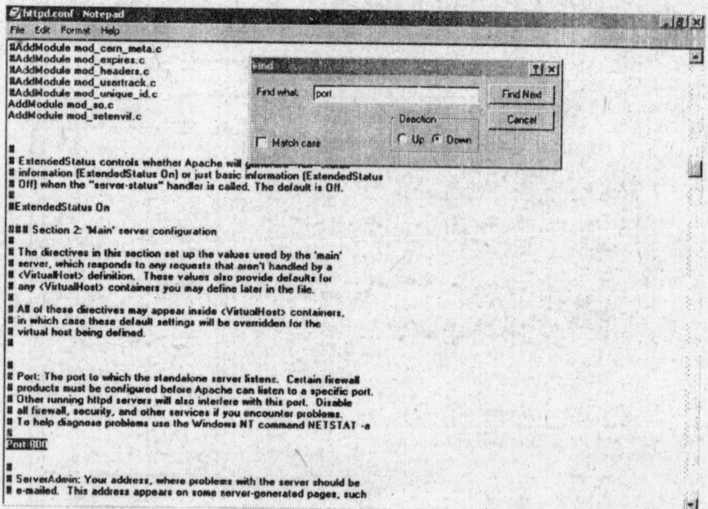

Fig 5.25

2. The file will be opened in Notepad Editor as shown in Fig 5.25. Click on Edit menu of Notepad, find for the word 'Port', as shown in Figure, change the port number from 80 to 800. After saving this file, you will find Apache running on port 800.

3. Restart HTTP Server by clicking **Start >> Programs** >> **Apache HTTP Server >> Control Apache Server**, then clicking on **Restart**

4. Test by typing in the browser http://localhost:800/ or by http://suresh:800/
5. You should be able to see the welcome screen of Apache Web Server, if you can see then you are successfully changed the port number.

Web Site Hosting and Management

After Installation of web server, your job is to host a web site and learning about web hosting & its management. There are various ways to host your web site. You can choose either options No.1 or option No. 2 given below: -

1. You can host your web site at an ISP's (Internet service provider) server. (e.g. ERNET, VSNL, Satyam).

   In this case, ISP will provide you the space and necessary maintenance [& domain name may also be provided, if available]. You can update your site regularly by uploading the pages. ISP will charge for hosting and other services in this case. In the case of Web server hosting with the ISP, ISP owns and maintains a firm's Web server and supports all traffic. Firms need not invest in server hardware or worry about high-speed leased lines to support the Web traffic.

2. Alternatively, You can host the web at your end at one local Server, if you do so, you have to follow these steps:

    a) You must be having a dedicated connectivity with a set of IP numbers for the machines. You will get these IP numbers, from ISP.

    b) You can register your domain name with some domain-registering agency (e.g. you can take *.ac* domain). In that case your domain name will be like "your_university.ac.in", if you want to register your domain under "in" domain, you will be required contact to NCST, Mumbai. NCST is a agency that provide the domain name under "in" domain. Visit the site http://domain.ncst.ernet.in/ for more information or send an e-mail to domain@ncst.ernet.in. For domain .in, which is meant for our country NCST (domain.ncst.ernet.in) is an authorised body. NCST has been involved in registering domain names under .in domain name space since 1995.

    c) Installation and Configuration of web server with registered IP at your place.

    d) Creating or Uploading your pages to your web serve and publishing them.

Useful URLs

(Used in this chapter and for further reading)

(All Accessed on Nov. 16, 2003)

1. Netcraft Web Site http://www.netcraft.com
2. Microsoft Web Site http://www.microsoft.com/
3. Netscape Web Site http://www.netscape.com
4. IIS Help on Localhost http://localhost/iisHelp/
5. Apache Web Site http://www.apache.org http://www.apache.org/dist/httpd/
6. Domain Registration : Indian Domain Name Registration http://domain.ncst.ernet.in/

CHAPTER 6

Designing Library Web Site

"Imagination is more important than knowledge."
-Albert Einstein

Objective

This chapter is specifically aimed towards librarians and library staff involved in World Wide Web management, and also as a guidance to the designers of library web page.

Well, first of all, you should have a web site, if you don't have, then you are missing some essential IT methods to serve your library users.

'Website designing and management' definitely may be a suitable title of a workshop or training programme. However, you may be surprised to discover that, a web page creation is inherently an easy task today, with availability of lots of tools. As you know that the purpose of the Library web site is to provide "authentic and structured information on *library services*".

Library services includes access rules to library, opening hours and contacts, access to electronic services and databases etc. If you have subscribed to some full-text journals, then most probably you would like to assist users, by developing a web-based, searchable database of full-text e-journals (and also of newspaper titles), and obviously from your Library WEB SITE!!! Therefore, presence of Library on the web is a useful feature to the users.

By the time you finish this chapter, you will be ready to start creating a web site for your library. Although the structure and contents of a library web site may vary from library to library, participants in all library web projects need to know the concepts and terminology involved, and also required to ensure a high profile of the Library on a University Intranet System.

Need

We know that a web site is the electronic face of the Library. Like all other Library services, the web site must continually grow well, with time to meet new demands and use technology to provide the best possible services.

However, the librarian need not learn HTML and other skills himself for creating a page, instead he should know less-technical issues, such as- selecting a web-hosting service, announcement and evaluation of a library web site, motivating his staff to get a training on internet & web and also to buy good quality books to improve the web designing skills of information personnel working for library web project/university Internet project.

Librarians involved with the development of a simple library-oriented web site will admit that they needs to understand *how web documents are created and structured.* If they are not aware then they will find themselves caught in a difficult situation, if in case they have to attend a technical meeting.

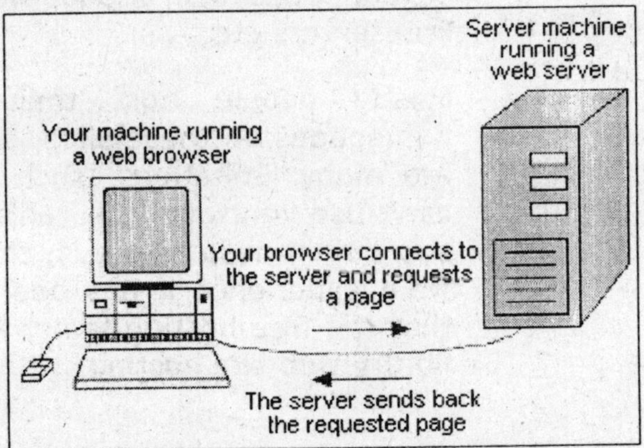

Fig. 6.1 Source: www.howstuffworks.com

It should be observed that while HTML skills are needed for a web designer or Webmaster. A web developer is required to have knowledge of HTML tags, creation of tables, images, frames, adding audio/ video to a web page, dynamic HTML, inclusion of graphics, CSS, also programming e.g. Java scripts etc. But these skills are not the necessary skills to be learnt by librarians; instead they must understand the general principles of creating and maintaining web contents, and also about what contents should go into which page and overall structure of subsequent pages. Meanwhile, it would be meaningful to look into the Fig 6.1 to learn how an HTML page travels from web server to user's browser.

No Free Hosting

You may be aware that there are many free sites available on the World Wide Web to host web contents. Some of the examples include Geocities, Tripod, Netfirms, Freeservers etc.

Mostly people host their small homepages on these sites, as there are many limitations [such as you can't use your own cgi, can't create sub directories etc etc...], therefore from experience it has been found that the free hosting is not fit for a library web site hosting.

Power of the Web

The Web is a powerful way to disseminate information quickly, clear from the fact that many recruiters these days publish advertisements on Employment news and other newspapers with a string attached to refer to their website for complete details.

The power of the Web lies in the ability to jump from one place to another place in cyberspace using "hypertext". This hyper-linking of resources creates an electronic web of interconnecting computers around the world, hence the "World Wide" Web. Connectivity is achieved through the use of the Hypertext Transfer Protocol (HTTP) and the Hypertext Markup Language (HTML). Of course, we have deliberately left out a lot of details and some tricks of HTML you should know, but that can be grasped easily by studying any book on HTML coding.

Issues

The matters of copyright and the Internet publishing are quit complex, wide and even unclear.

There are many other issues librarians creating Web content need to be concerned about.

Usefulness & Hits

The true purpose of developing and launching of website is achieved only when it is visited by the intended audience (users of the library). It's up to you to decide what is best for your visitors. You can even make a survey.

The number of 'hits' being received by a website, can be counted and website traffic can be analysed. Once you have determined that people are indeed visiting your Library Web site, the next step is to identify where they come from and which pages they are viewing.

After determining what content is popular, and what contents are being ignored, one can tailor contents to satisfy visitors.
Users of the site differ in following criteria:-

- The type of information they are looking.
- In the level of technology they are using,
- Their cultural background &

demographic level, skill level,

- And prior experience with web

A more detailed analysis of your web site traffic will assist you in improving your service on the Web, which in turn increases the traffic to your web site. [The information about your web site traffic generally comes from web server log files.]

Tools

There are several good *W Y S I W Y G* HTML editors available, that use many of the same buttons and conventions as common to word processors. *WYSIWYG* stands for "What You See Is What You Get".

Netscape Composer, Microsoft's FrontPage are popular products, however a web page can be developed in Notepad also.

If the applications you currently use are Microsoft Office, you can also generate web pages. In particular, by using MS-Office (Word) one can very easily generate basic HTML pages, and can even turn existing Word documents into HTML.

You can even develop Shockwave Flash files and put them on your website, but you have to consider the time of downloading as it might cause delay in downloading and also require plug-ins installed at the user machine.

General considerations

- Purpose? - what is true intention for building web system to take advantages?
- Audience? - who act as audience? Remember that once your web site is launched, it is your responsibility to collect feed back and before that fulfilling the information need of audience and keeping then happy by providing appropriate e-contents.

Staff? - what will be the team size and who will be the team members. The safest way is to find enthusiastic people in your team and to decide upon main things such as:-

1. Who will work on the web site?
2. What will be the development time?
3. Allocation of responsibilities?

Now, it would be fair to decide upon the contents of your web pages. Even it you are familiar with the issues, we recommend going through this chapter before tackling the rest of book.

Design Step 1: What should be there?
Library Home Page: - [Page 1 or Index page]

From here, we will start an in-depth discussion of a Library web site and its possible contents and with exemplary site of IIT Bombay as our model. (Considering the fact that IITB Library is pivotal in INDEST Consortium and with very common understanding of towering status of institution itself.)

So let's get started with first design issue: - Page1 is nothing but known as the home page or website. The web site's first page is often nominated as index.html. The hyperlinks to other pages can be presented either using "buttons" or as text links. Buttons are small images (often in gif format) and they act as links to subsequent web pages. Design your pages as a collection of several succinct pages, like chapters in a book, each focused to a particular topic for quick information and efficient browsing by the user. Then use hyperlinks to organise that collection. Each library page should be dated and signed to show when the page has been created/ updated and who is responsible for it. From page 1 (Index page), the following links should be provided to go to other pages.

- (Link to) "**About**" itself
- (Link to) "**What is new...**" (page)or current awareness (page)
- (Link to) "**Services**" (page)
- (Link to) "**Collections**" (page)
- (Link to) "**Databases**" (page)
- (Link to) "**Digital Library**" (Page)
- (Link to) "**Download** (Page)
- (Link to) "**Contact information**" (page) or "Email to webmaster"
- (Link to) the **Internet** or **"Intranet"** web (page of parent organisation)

- (Links to) "**Other libraries**" (web sites or pages)

We shall discuss all these links one by one and observe each page content. We take a sample web site for our study. For example, you can visit the structured web site of IIT Bombay. The *Central library Home page (*of IIT Bombay) is shown in Fig. 7.2

In addition to below, (as shown in fig. 6.2) the **additional links such as -**

(Link to) **Downloads** (page),

(Link to) **Search** (page),

(Link to) **Digital Library** (page),

(Link to) **Access to e-journals** etc

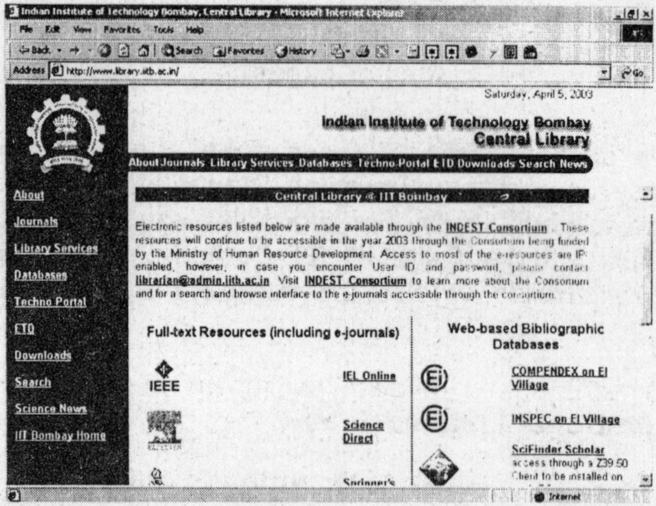

Fig. 6.2 Index (Main) page of IIT Bombay Library

-can also be provided.

Our next question from the series of links is about "What matter or content should go into subsequent web pages?".

1. We take "**About"** first. If a user clicks on the link **About,** he or she shall be moved to a subordinate page (most probably nominated as about.htm) containing name of the library, a logo or a scanned photograph, and a list of library activities along with a short description of the library.

2. The Second link may be "**What's new"** and should move users to new.htm containing latest 'library news'. Each news item should be dated, and no old news items should be present (new information only).

3. Third link may be **"Services".** As the user clicks on this link, he or she will be moved to the page containing information about services, on the services page, probably nominated as *services.htm*. Information on user limitations or rights should be included.

As shown in Figure 6.3, you can provide short information about the Library services, policies, bibliographic tools, catalogues, databases, some subject guides for research scholars, information about trainings, various refresher courses, current awareness (what's new), electronic submission of feedbacks from users and so on.

From this page, several links to other consequent web pages can be provided. As shown in IIT Bombay services page in Fig 6.4.

3(a) Borrowing instructions: - who is allowed to borrow material, which material and on which terms.

3(b) Renewal of loans:- This page is needed if the renewal of loans may be done using a web interface to the library system.

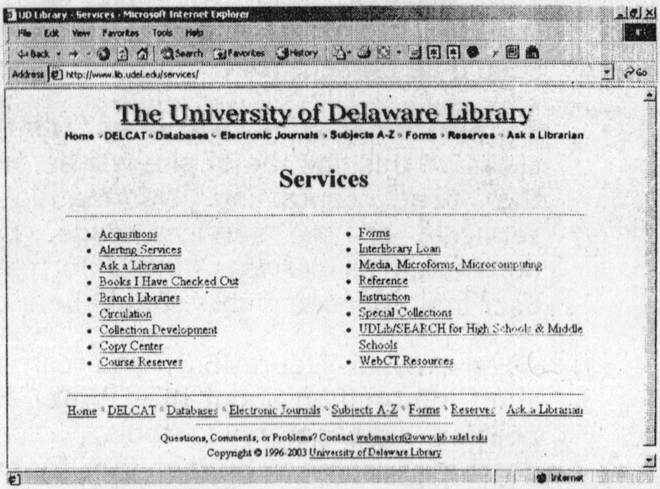

Fig. 6.3 Services page to the University of Delaware Library

3 (c) OPAC:- If OPAC is there, it should be provided as shown in Fig 7.4.

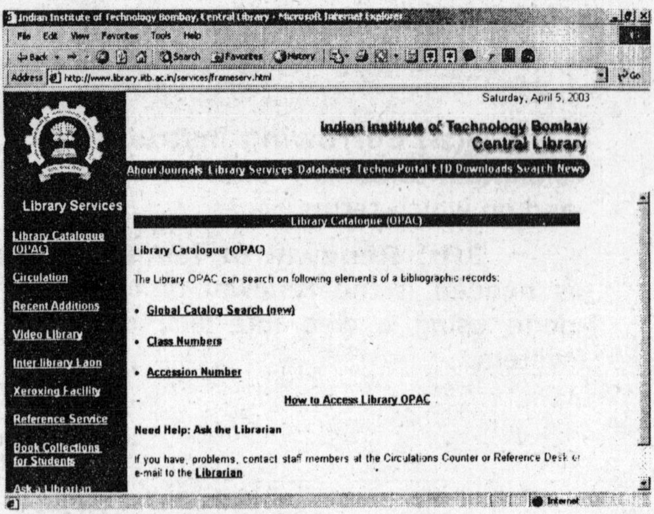

Fig. 6.4 OPAC Page

3 (d) Video-Library: - The value of content is much if supplemented by videos.

3 (e) Inter-Library Loans: - Schemes and procedures for Inter-Library loan are explained on this page, and it can be under the Services.

3 (f) Document delivery services:- Information on Books, journal articles, conference papers etc, material, which are not available in the library, and how one can access to them using DDS. If the library provides a service then the service can be described here..

3(g) Ask a Librarian: - If an answer service is available from library's end, then some query form (e-mail) or feedback form can be provided.

3(h) Techno-Portal: - If some techno-portal exists, then it may be included under the services.

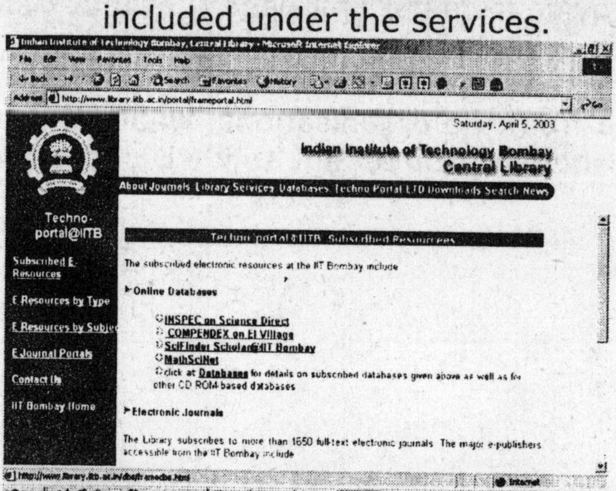

Fig. 6.5 Techno-Portal Page

4. Collections:- Depending on your situation, you may now be ready to describe the invaluable library collection. If there are databases online for reference, there should a link in the text to the relevant database.

5. Databases:- One of the hot topics in the world of web is "web-enabled-database" or "database-backed pages" or "dynamic" pages. If the Library has developed databases of structured data and approved users to access, then all the databases may get a link from Index Page. And further, several resources of online databases can be organised under the page online.htm. The name of a database acts as a link to the database. A short description of the databases together with access rights should be provided.

6. Digital Library:- If there is a provision of digital library system inside a traditional library and special documents are available then, the link may be provide from the first page (i.e. Index Page).

If Digital Library is so important then it can even be linked from the organisational web site [e.g. DRTC Web site has a Direct link to it's Digital Library.]

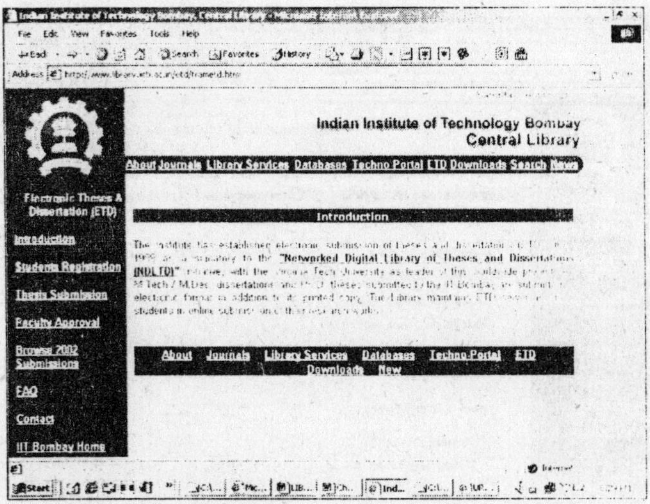

Fig. 6.6 Digital Library page of IIT Bombay

7. Download:- One can organise various forms, lists, information, free softwares and utilities to be downloaded from library website at this page, download.htm.

The download page is generally considered a popular page on the web site of a Library.

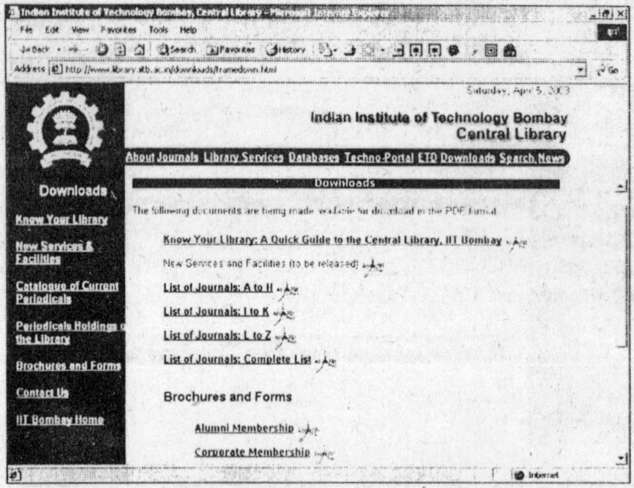

Fig. 6.7 Download page of IIT Bombay

8. Contact information:-This page contact.htm could contain the following information: address information, opening hours, staff of the library. So it, someone who is facing a problem or have a query can meet suitable staff member concerned. page providing staff bio-details, designations and their concerned works.

Design Step 2:-
What should be the structure?

We urge you to divide the information (you are about to publish) into subdocuments (individual HTML-documents). Link all the subdocumentss into a tree- structure showing which subdocument will be under another subdocument and there should always be a link from every subdocument to the index or home page. Don't put too much text and images in one document. Remember that 'Less is best, on screen' as reading on the screen is different from reading on paper. Just two or three clicks down, the user should be able to locate the information. It means that you shouldn't make the tree too deep. Give a name to each document (file). The name of a document should describe the content of that document, like in the picture above. First document (i.e. home page) is usually named *index.htm*

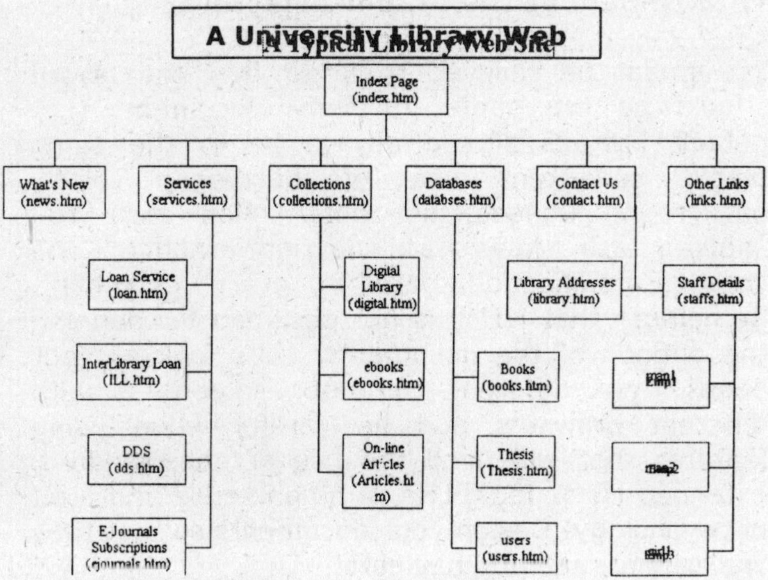

Fig. 6.8. A sample example chart of structure of web pages of a University library

You can save your HTML files and images in an unorganised way as it ultimately depends upon you. For example...in one single directory on your web server, but if there are lots of files, you need to learn how to maintain the files and how to organise them into subdirectories.... otherwise maintenance will become quite tough. Fig 7.8 attempts to show the hierarchy of web pages.

Images belonging to only one document should be placed in the same directory with the document file itself.

Design Step 3
What should be the Graphical lay-out?

You might be relieved to know that the layout should be the same in every document, (i.e. default buttons should always be in the same place, consistent use of headings, colors, background images, horizontal rules etc.) You should also have a copyright notice and creation/modification date in every document. Remember that HTML is not designed for defining the outlook of the documents. Let's look at your pages from different computer screens & with different browsers and be careful when using features that will need the use of non-standard, extended HTML tags. Use common sense and a bit of psychology. Design your documents so that they are easy to read and navigate.

Design Step 4
HTML tools selection

Make sure that the documents you are going to publish on the web are already in electronic form, (say in word format) and then you have a converted them to HTML file formats. Some information may be lost during conversion, (e.g.

multiple columns in original document cannot be translated into HTML). Tables and images are also sometimes difficult for some converters. In most cases, converted files need some manual editing. See and correct them.

HTML files can be written with any text editor, but HTML editors (Example: FrontPage from Microsoft) have powerful menus and buttons supporting HTML coding. Even when using a WYSIWYG drag-and-drop editor you should prompt your designers to know what elements you can have in HTML document & learn advance web design.

Design Step 5
Testing web pages

Once the pages are uploaded on your server, it is time to test. There are several points mentioned in the check-list mentioned below: -

Check List: -

1. Ensure that the web slte reflects the library's position within the University.
2. The web site conveys a professional image with an informational focus.
3. Web pages are tested, and meet, accessibility standards. Make it simple and sparse.
4. Go and see that the web site is mounted on a stable system and is well supported.

5. Check that the homepage is an efficient gateway to the site.
6. Also verify that the web pages metadata standards & easy to search. Web pages have accurate titles and meaningful URLs.
7. Ensure that Information on the web site is current.
8. Verify that it is easy for users to find link to parent page (or 'Home').
9. Verify that users easily understand language used.
10. Ensure that proper system encourages feedback from users used to continually improve the site.
11. Take pain to actively promote the web site among Library users.
12. The Web Site follows copyright rules.
13. Remember that it is an iterative process.

Design Step 6
Announcing web pages

After you have finished designing & testing your web-documents and you think that they are ready to be published, you can submit your site's URL to some announcement site, or search engine.

You can also write to newsgroups about your site. Remember the netiquette when writing to the newsgroups.

Announcing of your site can be one on there resources

- Mailing List
- News groups
- Search Engines

Design Step 7
Develop the trust

1. Publish a monthly newsletter of your organisation. Create a relationship with the reader.
2. Produce excellent content and update them timely to generate web site loyalty.
3. Add a discussion board, it possible.
4. Try to, provide WebOPAC on Internet.

Design Step 8
Maintenance

Maintenance though last in the cycle is the most important. If you don't maintain your documents, you have killed your time. It's as important as building. Check that your links work, remove outdated information. Tools for maintaining links etc. can be found in many shareware collections. Some of your team members can be given the responsibility to maintain the pages, while Webmaster will ensure that web server is publishing the pages. The last but not the least "Learn from experience".

Useful URLs

(Used in this chapter and for further reading)

(All Accessed on Nov. 16, 2003)

1. How Stuff Works Web site http://www.howstuffworks.com
2. Tripod Web site http://www.tripod.com
3. Geocities Web site http://www.geocities.com
4. FreeServers Web sitehttp://www.freeservers.com
5. Netfirws Web site http://www.netfirms.com
6. Microsoft Front Page http://www.microsoftfrontpage.com
7. IIT Bombay Library Web sitehttp://www.library.iitb.ac.in
8. University of Delaware Library Web site http://www.lib.udel.edu/services/
9. DRTC http://drtc.isibang.ac.in

CHAPTER 7

How to Make your First Digital Library

"The empires of the future are empires of the mind"

-- Winston Churchill

Purpose:

In this chapter, first of all, we will discuss some of the important issues relating to digital libraries. After that we will move very quickly to develop our own Digital Library in a very short span of time experimenting with a windows-based open source software known as Greenstone. However, only the major issues will be covered in the chapter. You will find this chapter more interesting and useful, if you follow the suggested sequence on the computer. In this chapter, step-by-step procedures are depicted to develop digital collections by using a software utility Greenstone. It is well said by Greenstone.org, "This software provides a new way of organising information and publishing it on the Internet or on CD-ROM".

We have already learnt using apache as a web server under windows operating system. After reading this chapter, you will find that building a

Digital Library is a real joy. It is to hope that this chapter will encourage you for effective development of a Digital Library and put your digital collections into public domain.

Well, there are lots of alternative softwares available and by using any one of them one can build a model of Digital Library. You have to analyse your requirements and answer, which type of Digital Library you are going to develop, will it be a collection of ebooks? Or will be a collection of PDF? or Word Documents ?

Digital libraries; connected with a Library Portal, - which also provides search facility to digital collections, in addition to other sorts of resources; provides the necessary happy feelings to library users. This implies: that they can avail a variety of services and information anytime using Campus LAN or from Internet (if you put digital collections on the Web).

Ensure that all your digital collections are placed in the secured area of your Library Website. Don't hesitate to take help from computer experts from the Computer Science Department located near by. By describing, the design and implementation processes, user's perspective, librarian's perspectives and developer's viewpoints, we intend to educate the reader about Digital Library, key design issues, latest know-how, implementation process, and at last development of a sample collection of PDF files.

An Overview

A Digital Library can be thought of as a collection of files, which is stored and accessed electronically. A Digital Library must have a user-friendly interface as shown in figure 7.1 and ease of use, and if possible, the web site should be accessible. In some of the cases, Digital Library is the foundation of your library site and the other features are added to create a portal, while in other cases sites are basically portals and Digital Library is included at a later stage.

As a matter of fact, the "World Wide Web" service is a part of the Internet (as already explained in previous chapter), has been so popular and is very powerful too, it embodies audio, video, text, and animations, and therefore it is the medium to be preferred to deliver digital contents. By many other methods (mobile, PDAs.) one can access a website, if it exists. A website may also be used to provide 'Distance Education" or for online course delivery.

User's Perspective:

One reason for the user to be impressed, by a 'Digital Library' is that because of his need and for quick information is met and since great searching facility offered by digital archives and collections ease his tasks. A friendly interface, giving him 24 hours access from any corner of the campus is responsible to ensure popularity.

Imagine a situation where a user wishes to use a 'Digital Library' because of its simplicity and as a central location for accessing information on a particular topic e.g. on "Computer Science".

Now further suppose that the user searched for "SQL Server" and he gets results for "Operating System"; this greatly mismatched answer-set for his query will lead to a big disappointment while the user gets irritated or loses faith in the system.

Therefore, common sense leads us to make a simple rule of thumb that "a Digital Library must keep topics separate into logical directories, and subdirectories", otherwise it would be totally useless. In other words, a Digital Library should also have a user interface, which is easy to use, and reasonable to navigate, and is divided into various subsections.

Even, an interesting point to note is that many people seem to be confused and think that an automated library is a digitised one. However, An automated library is not necessarily a 'Digital Library'. This automation does not make it "digital" in the sense we see here.

However, it is true that a 'Digital Library', must first be automated in order to deliver its impact over the community. There are two possibilities: First, where a library that contains material in digitised form (converted from other sources), and second where a library that contains digital material (which are borne digital).

Both are different and if understood properly, no confusion arises. In simple words, it can be said that a Digital Library provides services from digital resources, which are either both developed and available in digital form or converted from non-digital print resources e.g. books.

A Digital Library can be a Virtual Library (Library Without walls) if it exists only virtually and the library does not have any physical collection. Whereas a hybrid library is a combination of traditional and Digital Library, where both electronic and print resources are used alongside each other.

Librarian's Perspective

According to great ancient Indian philosopher Patanjali "When you are inspired by some great purpose, some extraordinary project, all your thoughts break their bonds: your mind transcends limitations, your consciousness expands in every direction, and you find yourself in a new, great and wonderful world. Dormant forces, faculties and talents become alive, and you discover yourself to be a greater person by far than you ever dreamed yourself to be". Undoubtedly, development of a Digital Library is fascinating extraordinary project and has a great purpose for Library Professionals & LIS students. Therefore, a Digital Library project emerges as an most important activity for librarians.

Digital Library has awarded new methods & facilities to library staffs, consider an example: In a traditional library the book issue process is quite lengthy as it involves right from the user's- request followed by removal of a book from a shelf and issuing it out. But in case of a fully Digital Library, because the "book" is available in digitised form, it can be copied to a user's computer for reading or can be sent though email; but still it remains in the computer "stacks," and therefore, it can immediately be "issued" to another user. This will lead to a conclusion that holds (reservations) theory has become a thing of the past for a fully Digital Library, at the expense of a very complex and efficient software system. Digital Library can even help you to partner with campus academicians to provide contents.

Mary L. Kao writes in her book '*Introduction to Technical Services for Library Technologies' that " More and more electronic resources will be collected by libraries. Cataloging rules will be modified to suit the electronic environment, or different rules, such as the Dublin Core, will be adopted universally for cataloging electronic materials. Library collections will include e-books, e-journals, and Internet resources."* Therefore, it is to deduce that, very clearly digital collections would be a part of a future library, containing e-books, e-journals etc-etc.

It has already been observed that developments in IT, Computer and Telecommunication have been affecting libraries of all types; the challenges are rapid for libraries and their staffs. The outcome and integration of digital objects, Internet access, e-journals, search engines, and library automation systems, is overwhelming but causing confusion and forcing information officers, and librarians to rethink about their working styles, goals and modes of operations in 21st century.

However, it may be a proud for a librarian to have a 'Digital Library' today, but as a matter of fact, the job-role of the libraries in a digital world is uncertain and challenging. How libraries respond to the implicated challenging situation evolved by the advent of the computer and the proliferation of cheaper, faster and more efficient means of accessing information will have an impact in their retention. A Librarian is rapidly being thought of as Knowledge managers or content managers.

Various issues involving piracy of contents, copyright, privacy and knowledge management are also of major concerns for librarians in today's computerised world.

Librarians and publishers are under stress of learning new methods, and finally have felt that their services and roles are changing in a digital world and their management and users requirements are challenging and diverse. It can even go to the extent of disappointment. There is a consensus that some type of electronic information management is required and it is in fact the right way to the future. Therefore, electronic publication system will evolve and it leads to question like where it will finally lead to. Electronic publications are managed by a 'Digital Library System' and archived for users. Digital

Library is a set of documents developed and indexed by sets of programs or software. Also it requires technology to link various resources. There are several software available to create a Digital Library: -some are free while others charges mercilessly. The Greenstone Digital Library Software is a popular free software for libraries. It is distributed in collaboration with UNESCO. It can be downloaded from Greenstone's Website; it has close connections with NZDL (New Zealand Digital Library).

To see a real example of implementation by an Indian organisation, you are advised to please visit www.indialabourarchive.org, whose name is also mentioned on website of Greenstone (www.greenstone.org).

Other examples of this type of digital library implementations in India include DRTC Digital Library, NCSI-IISC Demo Collection and are available on web sites https://drtc.isibang.ac.in/ and http://144.16.72.189/cgi-bin/library.exe respectively.

Developer's Perspective

A 'Digital Library' is not the same as a website. One may think that 'obviously there is no difference between the web and digital library, whatever I put should be visible over the network'. But in fact, the library philosophy tells us that whenever a library system get a new material, it is treated as an important entity and added or integrated to its existing collection without having to edit it or doing any manual work. Once added, the new material becomes a source of reference and a property of library immediately, and it will be treated as a part of the existing collection. Talking digitally, it should be searchable and browsable; due to the searching from metadata, key words and text.

A developer may note that there should be two separate sections of your proposed Digital Library: one open section for public users and second (authenticated administrator/ developer reviewed) section for editors or developers. The public-user open section may consist of on-line reading material intended to be referred by public users, who don't have permissions equal to Editors or Administrators.

One of the first design issues in the creation of a 'Digital Library' is to prepare a list of top-level requirements, technical points and views. This list may include what informational documents the library will contain, how that information will be generated, what audience the information is intended for, and how the data will be accessed?. Whether the digital information for the library should be gathered through on-line submissions? or the Administrator or Editors will upload it should also be thought of a clear plan must be worked out and developed before one starts designing and developing. Secondly, it should be decided by the developer whether he or she is going to develop software or going to use already developed software such as Greenstone, (or Dspace or E-print etc...etc...)

Before site development begins, solve another important issue- one of them is the location of the Digital Library. Obviously on the web server: - The web server must be available on the Internet (or Intranet as applicable) with the enough hard drive space, and the ability to handle the expected access load. If a PC is used, it should be a good P-IV machine with 300 MHz Speed. 10 GB of free disk space would be enough to start. This will give your library space to expand.

Once the location of webserver is decided, a web server must be chosen. Mostly, users are at ease with Windows Operating System. Here Windows NT or Windows 2000 can be used, if one is going to build it on Windows Platform.

Popular web servers for Windows operating system are Microsoft's Internet Information Server, Apache Web Server, and Netscape's Enterprise Server. Out of them, the first two have been already studied by as in chapter 5. If a non-windows machine is chosen, then there are many free web servers that can be downloaded from the web. Apache is one of them. In this chapter, we are going to use Apache Web Server on Windows Platform.

Which hardware / software should be used? is an important decision. There are a number of other issues, a developer should consider, before creating a Digital Library. One issue is of search facility, while the other is of File System versus Database System, whether your digital books or documents should be stored in a file system or in a

DBMS; all that needs to be decided prior to starting from point zero. As far as Greenstone is concerned, it will use file system to store files, it is not using DBMS to store files.

If a site is not flexible for enhancement or updation. days will be wasted; in case, you need to make small changes. If a site is not secure digitally, someone with extra know-how can corrupt or damage important data. There fore, the other very important issues are flexibility and security.

Maintaining the quality of the data in the Digital Library is also an issue. If a Digital Library accepts all submissions, it may contain useless information too. The way to solve this problem has already been suggested by having either the editors or administrators do authenticate the newly submitted information.

One important issue is the rapidly changing technology. It is important to keep an eye on the changes that are taking place for the Web technology and library domains. An example of this is the standard of Dublin Core. The Dublin Core is a 15-element metadata element set intended to facilitate discovery of electronic resources. Metadata is simply `data about data".

Finally, the most important issue is to find out team of right personnel to develop such a Digital Library. By keeping up to date with the latest technologies and standards, an enthusiastic person can create a digital library system and consequently the work may prove to be useful for thousands of users.

Development of a Digital Library using Greenstone Software

First thing to know is that Greenstone is a software, which help you to launch a digital library. It is an open source, and a multilingual package; produced by NZDL project at University of Waikato. Greenstone is distributed (free of cost) in cooperation with UNESCO and Human Info, NGO. By using this, a library, or user can build a Digital Library on Windows (or Linux platform).

In developing countries, Digital Library is a sounding word and has become a buzzword. And many librarians are talking loudly about digital libraries and services in various conferences, seminars etc. This chapter will help you to come to a level with an idea to develop digital collections for your office or home, with a new thinking and new way of dissemination of your files.

A section of this chapter describes how to obtain associated software namely Apache and Activeperl; and how to install these software, followed by installation of Greenstone. All the three software are freely available from their websites.

Apache web server: Version: 1.3	This can be obtained from www.apache.org

Perl Language Version: 5.6	Active perl can be downloaded from www.activestate.com
Greenstone Software Version:2.39	This DL software can be downloaded form www.greenstone.org

Table 7.1

Installation Steps

1. Web Server You need an external web server such as Apache or IIS to publish your collection, and not the one, which is supplied along with Greenstone. Many large organisations already have a web server (on which, their web site exists). Apache is a very popular web server, and thus can now be used now by us to publish Digital Library collections. Installation process is very easy and since Installation of Apache has been already covered in chapter 5, so there is no need to repeat the installation process here again.

2. Perl To build collections with Greenstone you need the Perl language, version 5 or higher. For Windows, ActivePerl from *www.activestate.com can be downloaded and be used*. However, we are discussing this here for Windows machines only. A line for enthusiastic Linux Users who believe in experimentation and learning is that most Linux systems already have Perl installed but if not, then one can download necessary binaries and source code etc from perl.com.

3. Greenstone Download Greenstone from www.greenstone.org. The full-featured Greenstone software will run on 32-bit windows environment, such as Win Me, and NT/2000/Me. For Windows NT/2000 or Linux you have to log on as Administrator to configure a web server for Greenstone. You need not to just install binaries, run and enjoy.

Using this distribution, you may either install the "local library", or the "web library", or install and compile the source code. This distribution includes everything you need to run Greenstone (including a pre-built demonstration collection) and to build new Greenstone collections. This distribution uses a standard Windows installer program, simply download the file and double-click it to install as depicted in the following screens don't forget to download the additional reading material from the Greenstone web site. There are some greenstone guides, download them in a single directory for reading and reference purposes. Read them when you find some time or when you face problem

- Greenstone Digital Library Installer's Guide
- Greenstone Digital Library User's Guide
- Greenstone Digital Library Developer's Guide
- Greenstone Digital Library: From Paper to Collection

There are many issues that affect (or might affect) the installation procedure. Do you know how to reconfigure your webserver (Apache in our case) slightly to recognise the Greenstone software?

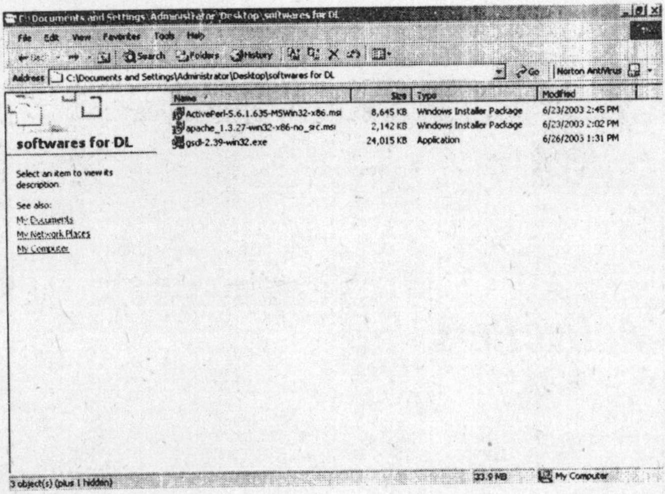

Fig. 7.1

Once you have downloaded the three files, you can collect them in a directory as shown in Fig 7.1. Since, it is assumed that you have already installed Apache, we now take the task of installing Perl in the system, which is already running the web server software. After installing Perl, we will install greenstone software. Fig 7.2 to 7.9 depicts the every step of installation with screen-shots, you can see in figures that a button 'Next' which is highlighted and has focus, needs a click to reach the next stage.

Fig 7.10 to 7.19 depicts the installation process of Greenstone software. The installation process is an easy task, mostly you would be required to click on the "Next" button, except sometime you need to provide requisite perimetric information (e.g. in Fig 7.16).

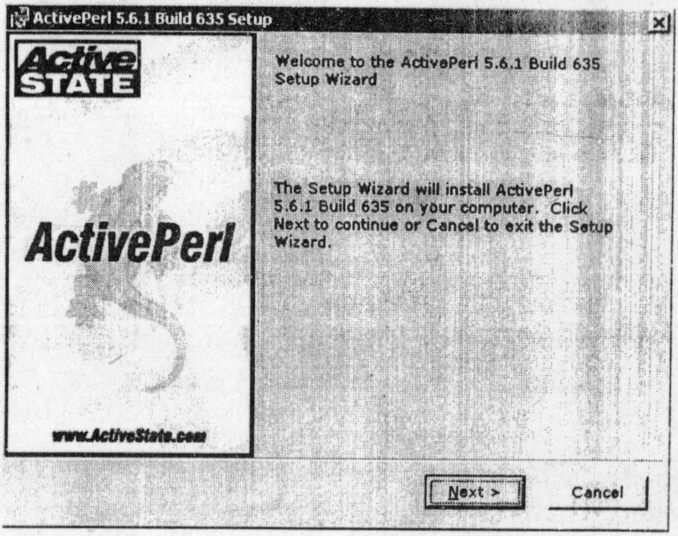

Fig. 7.2 Click on Next button

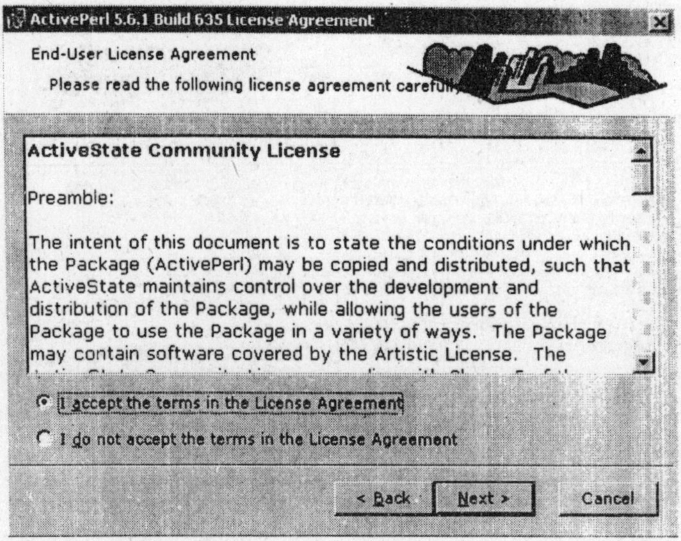

Fig. 7.3 Click on <u>Next</u> button

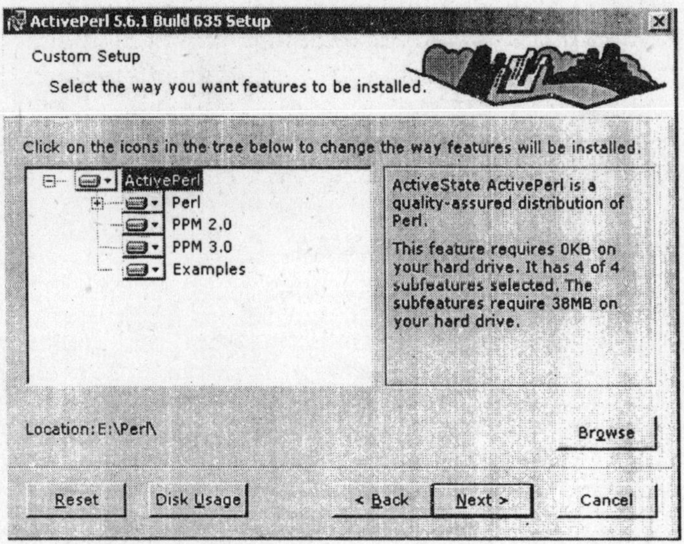

Fig. 7.4 Click on <u>Next</u> button

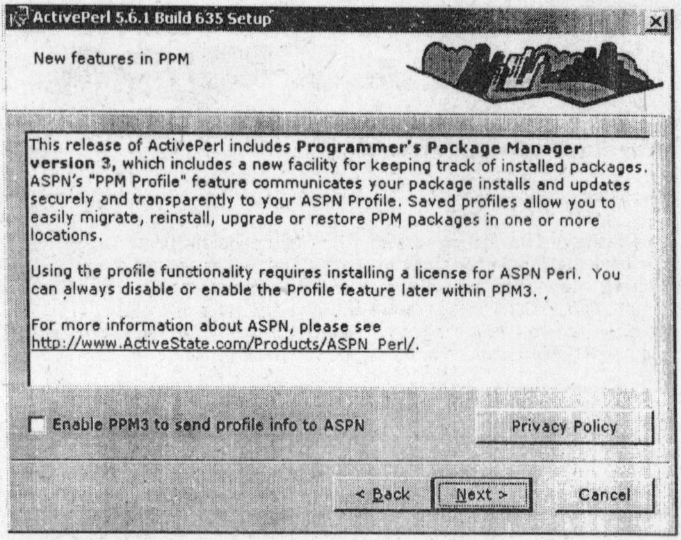

Fig. 7.5 Click on <u>Next</u> button

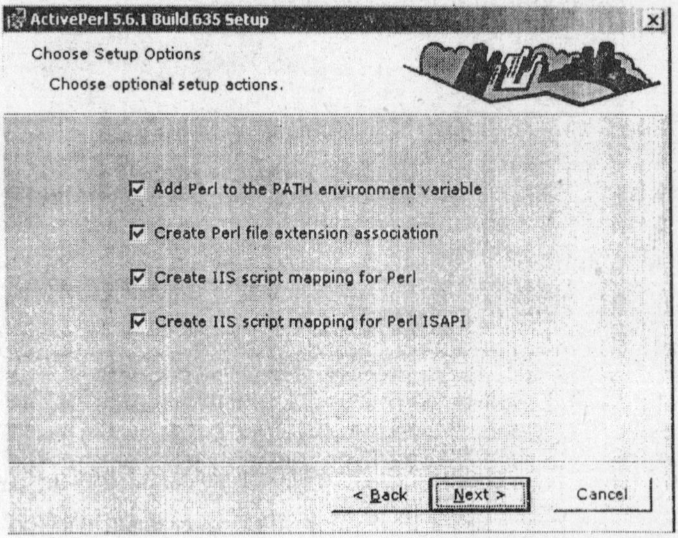

Fig. 7.6 Click on <u>Next</u> button

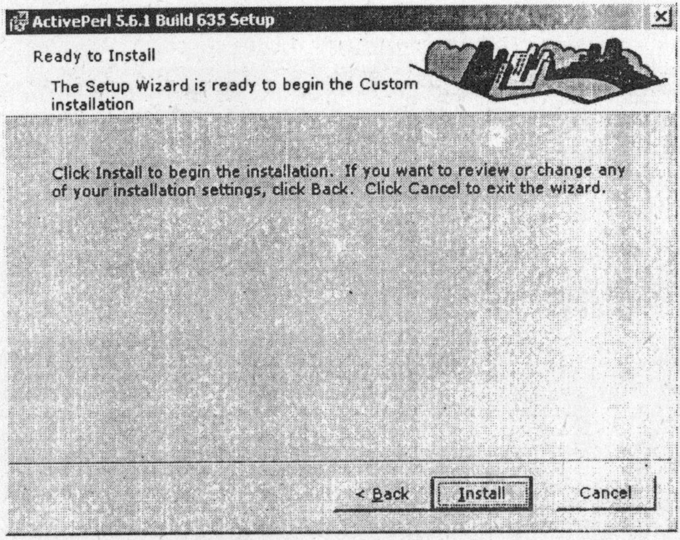

Fig. 7.7 Click on Next button

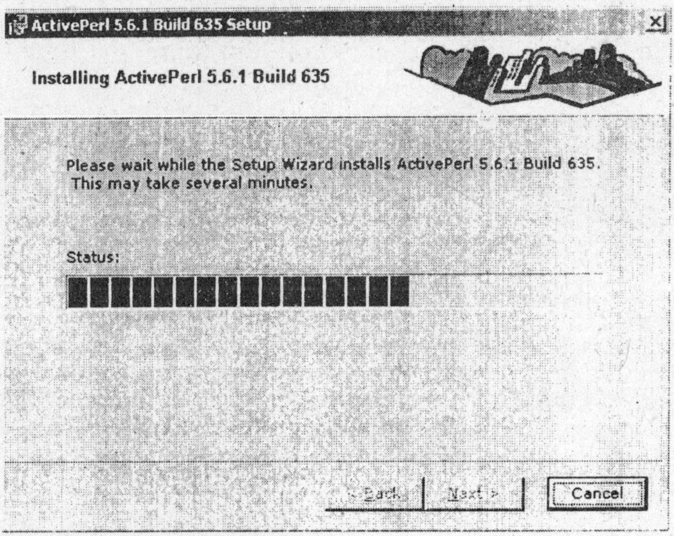

Fig. 7.8 A temporary screen

Fig. 7.9 Click on Finish button

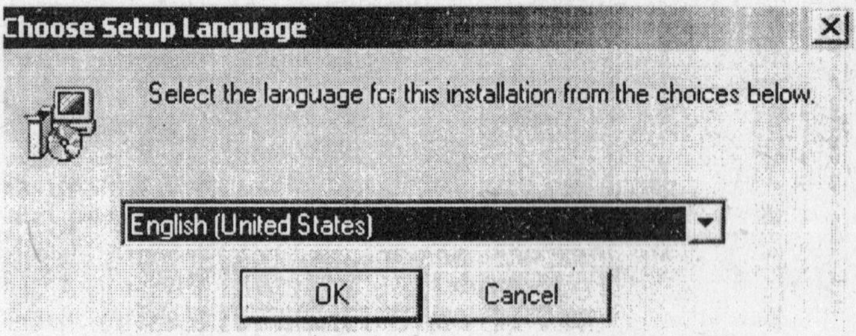

Fig. 7.10 Click on Ok button

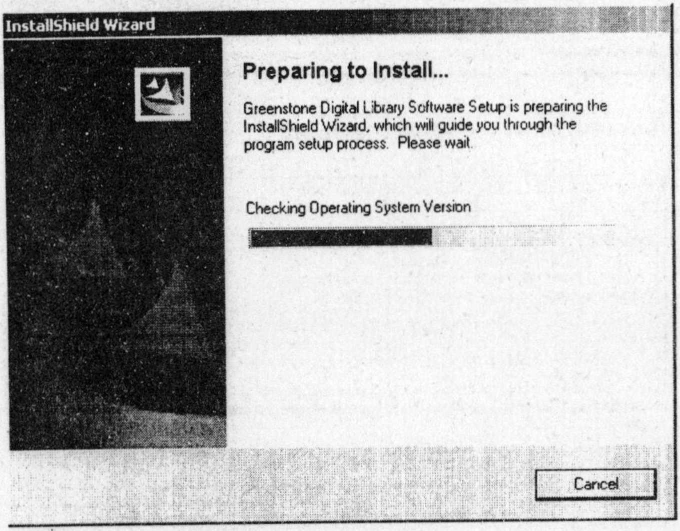

Fig. 7.11 A temporary screen

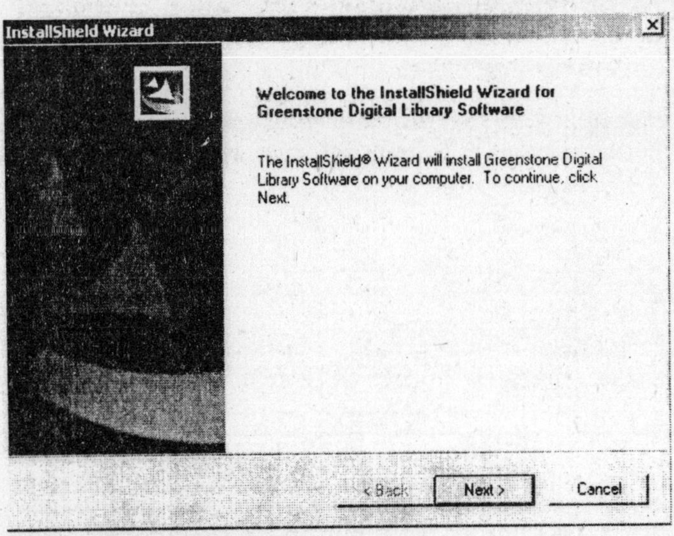

Fig. 7.12 Click on Next button

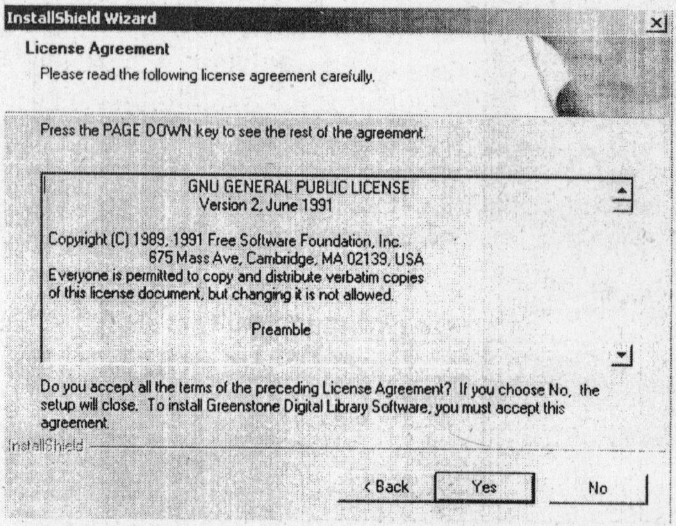

Fig. 7.13 Click on Yes button

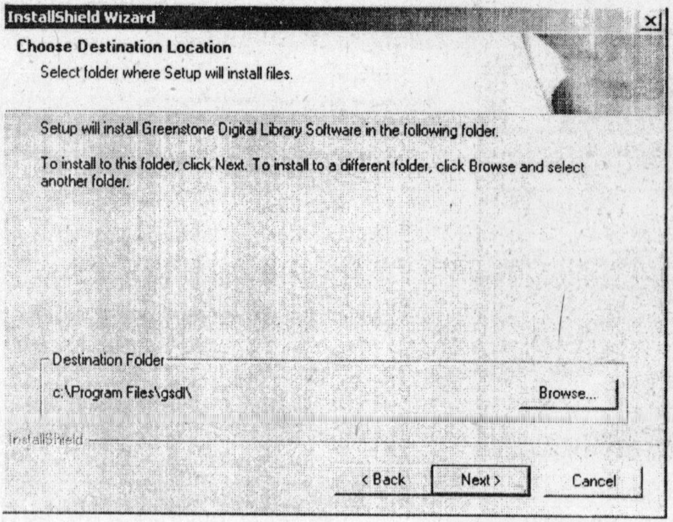

Fig. 7.14 Click on Next button

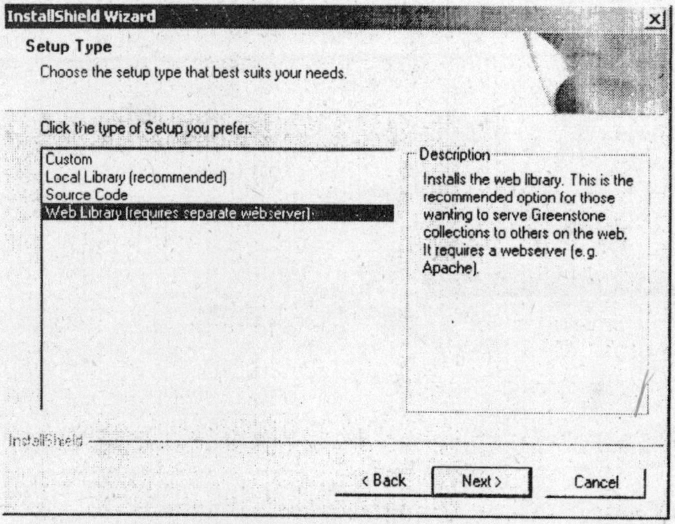

Fig. 7.15 Click on Next button

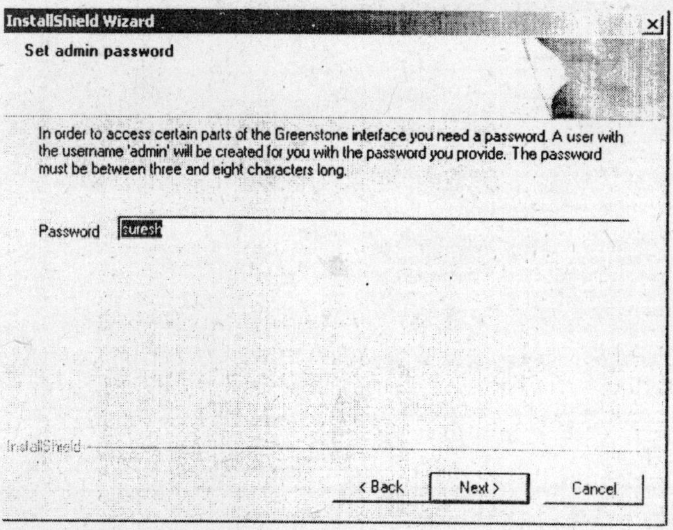

Fig. 7.16 Click on Next button

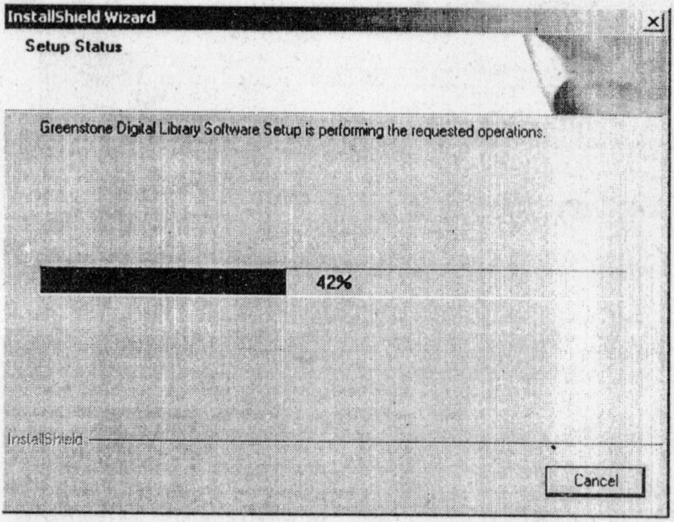

Fig. 7.17 A temporary screen

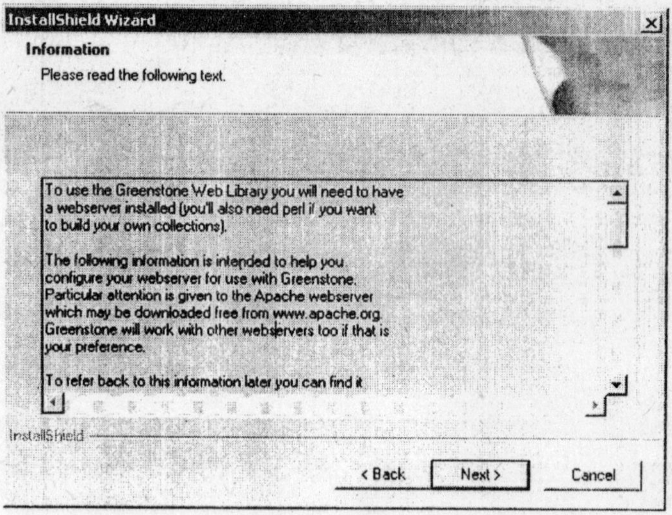

Fig. 7.18 Click on Next button

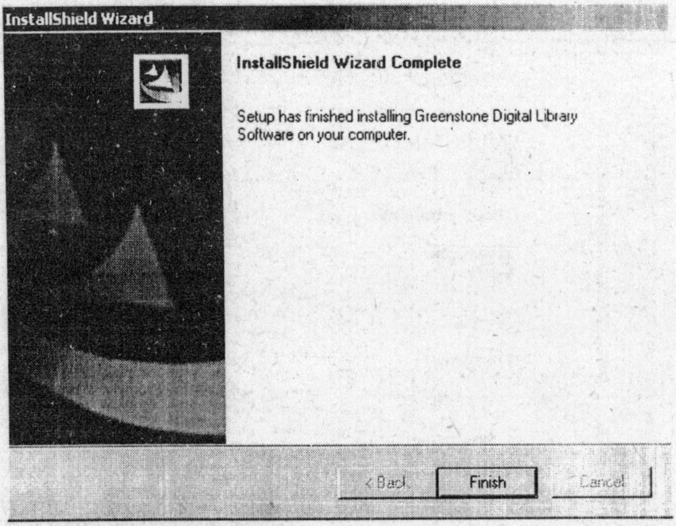

Fig. 7.19 Click on Finish button

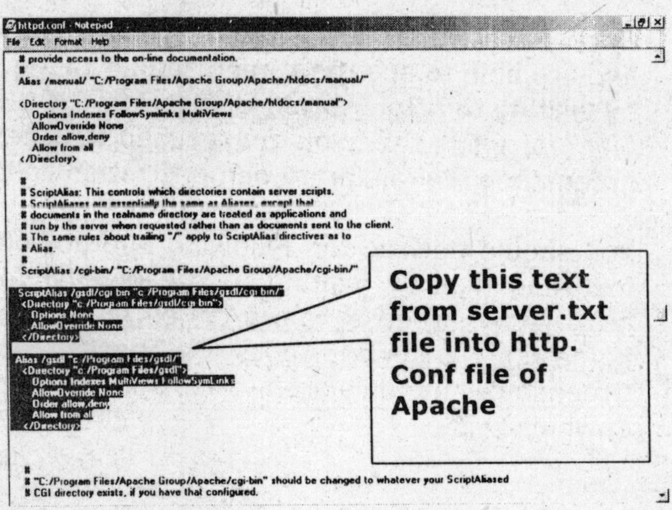

Fig. 7.20

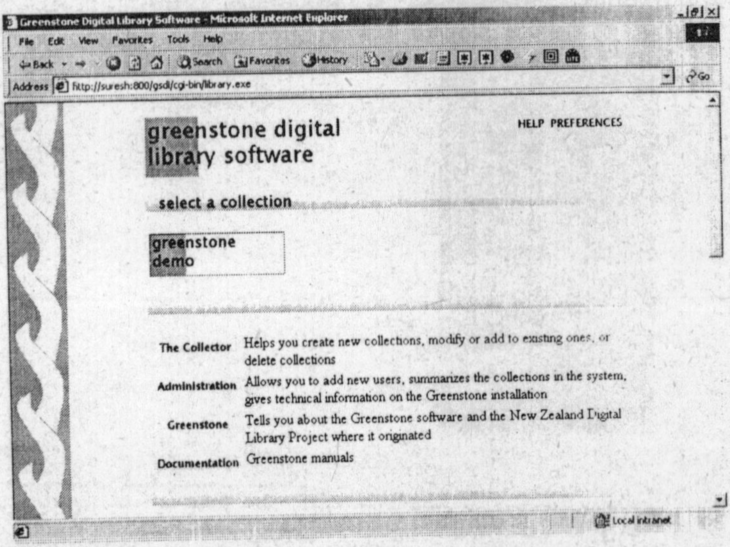

Fig 7.21

Once you have done the above exercises to install and are able to see the screen similar to Fig. 7.21, by visiting to <u>http://localhost/gsdl/cgi-bin/library.exe</u> then you are reached to access the greenstone digital library demonstration collection.

You should now do the following and download the following files by visiting to the given hyperlink:- <u>http://www.greenstone.org/cgi-bin/library?e=p-en-home-utfZz-8&a=p&p=docs</u>. These following Greenstone manuals are available in PDF format for download.

- **Installer's Guide**
- **User's Guide**

- **Developer's Guide**
- **From Paper to Collection**
- **Inside Greenstone Collections**

Once you have gone through these manuals and noted carefully what you have to do, you won't find any difficulty to configure the Greenstone Digital Library according to your needs.

As an experiment, you should try to develop a sample collection of these PDF files. Later, you can develop some useful collections for your readers.

Useful URLs

(Used in this chapter and for further reading)

(All Accessed on Nov. 16, 2003)

1. Apache Web Site http://httpd.apache.org/
2. ActiveState Web Site www.activestate.com
3. Greenstone Web Site http://www.grenstone.org
4. Dspace http://www.dspace.org/
5. Eprint http://www.eprints.org/
6. Inforlibrarian Web site http://www.infolibrarian.com
7. Indian Labour Archive http://www.indialabourarchive.org
8. DRTC http://drtc.isibang.ac.in/
9. New Zealand Digital Library http://www.nzdl.org

10. Humanity development library
 http://www.sadl.uleth.ca/nz/cgi-bin/library?a=p&p=about&c=hdl
11. Medical and health library
 http://www.sadl.uleth.ca/nz/cgi-bin/library?a=p&p=about&c=mhl
12. Agricultural information modules
 http://www.sadl.uleth.ca/nz/cgi-bin/library?a=p&p=about&c=aginfo
13. Commonwealth development library
 http://www.sadl.uleth.ca/nz/cgi-bin/library?a=p&p=about&c=cdl
14. Music library http://www.sadl.uleth.ca/musiclib
15. Bibliographic collection
 http://www.sadl uleth.ca/nz/cgi-bin/library?a=p&p=about&c=cltbib-e&ct=1&qt=1
16. Msword and pdf demonstration
 http://www.sadl.uleth.ca/nz/cgi-bin/library?a=p&p=about&c=wrdpdf-e
17. Marc Example http://www.sadl.uleth.ca/nz/cgi-bin/library?a=p&p=about&c=MARC-e
18. Simple image collection
 http://www.sadl.uleth.ca/nz/cgi-bin/library?a=p&p=about&c=image-e

Bibliography

Print Sources

1. Tanenbaum, Andrew S., *Computer Networks,* ed.3, Prentice-Hall of India, 1997.

2. Ackermann, Ernest C. and Hartman, Karen, *Searching and Researching on the Internet and the World Wide Web,* ed. 3, 2003.

3. Bradley, Phil, *The Advanced Internet Searcher's Handbook,* ed.1, Library Association Publishing, 1999.

4. Garett, David et al., *Intranets Unleashed,* ed.1, Techmedia, 1996.

5. Pandian, M Paul and Jambhekar, Ashok, *Internet for Libraries and Information Centres*, ed.1, Tata McGraw-Hill, 2001.

6. Waterhouse, Steve, *Building Intranets with Internet Information Server and FrontPage,* ed.1, Galgotia Publications, 1997.

7. Kao Mary L., *Introduction to Technical Services for Library Personnel,* ed.1, Jaico Publishing, 2003.

8. Kao Mary L., *Cataloging and Classification for Library Technicians,* ed.1, Jaico Publishing, 2003.

9. Ojala Marydee, *E-Content*, Dec 2000, 24(4):27.

Web Resources

1. Amazon http://www.amazon.com
2. Apache Web Site http://www.apache.org
3. DOT www.dotindia.com
4. ERNET Web Site http://www.ernet.in
5. Getting Started on the Internet http://www.imagescape.com/helpweb/
6. How Stuff Works http://www.howstuffworks.com
7. http://bones.med.ohio-state.edu/eric/papers/primer/copy.html
8. http://wdvl.com/
9. http://websearch.about.com/library/weekly/aa061903b.htm
10. http://www.academicinfo.net/refdirectories.html
11. http://www.acmebw.com/askmrdns/archive.php?category=81&question=149
12. http://www.ala.org/Content/NavigationMenu/ACRL/Publications/College and Research Libraries News/Back Issues 1998/July August6/Teaching Undergrads Web Evaluation.htm
13. http://www.ciol.com/content/news/repts/103040409.asp
14. http://www.ciol.com/content/special/internet/internetservices.asp
15. http://www.digital-librarian.com/internet.html
16. http://www.education-world.com/awards/past/2001/r0301-04.shtml
17. http://www.ir-ware.biz/wsl-ren.html
18. http://www.law.mercer.edu/career/CLE/cle996.htm
19. http://www.lib.berkeley.edu/TeachingLib/Guides/Evaluation.html
20. http://www.lib.berkeley.edu/TeachingLib/Guides/Internet/Evaluate.html
21. http://www.lib.berkeley.edu/TeachingLib/Guides/Internet/Evaluate.html
22. http://www.lib.berkeley.edu/TeachingLib/Guides/Internet/WhatIs.html
23. http://www.lib.udel.edu/services/
24. http://www.library.jhu.edu/elp/useit/evaluate/
25. http://www.llrx.com/features/engine3.htm

26. http://www.main.nc.us/search/specialtysearch.shtml
27. http://www.philb.com/countryse.htm#India
28. http://www.philb.com/webse.htm
29. http://www.sc.edu/beaufort/library/bones.html
30. http://www.sc.edu/beaufort/library/lesson1.html
31. http://www.sc.edu/beaufort/library/lesson2.html
32. http://www.sc.edu/beaufort/library/lesson3.html
33. http://www.sc.edu/beaufort/library/lesson4.html
34. http://www.sc.edu/beaufort/library/lesson5.html
35. http://www.sc.edu/beaufort/library/lesson5.html
36. http://www.sc.edu/beaufort/library/lesson6.html
37. http://www.webopedia.com/TERM/T/TCP_IP.html
38. http://www.zdnetindia.com/news/commentary/stories/6142.html
39. http://www2.widener.edu/Wolfgram-Memorial-Library/pyramid/goals5.htm
40. IISC Web Site http://iisc.ac.in
41. India Today Dec 2001 http://www.india-today.com/ctoday/20011201/net2.html
42. INFLIBNET web Site http://www.inflibnet.ac.in
43. Innovative Internet Applications in Libraries http://www.wiltonlibrary.org/innovate.html
44. Internet Guides http://library.berkeley.edu/TeachingLib/Guides/Internet/
45. Internet Society (ISOC) http://www.isoc.org/internet/history/cerf.shtml
46. Introduction to Internet http://www.pages.drexel.edu/~mbp24/course/Interint.htm
47. IPL http://www.ipl.org
48. ISPAI www.ispai.com/
49. Library of Congress http://www.loc.gov
50. Library Web Manager' s Reference Centre(DL SunSITE) http://sunsite.berkeley.edu/Web4Lib/RefCenter/
51. LookOff http://www.lookoff.com
52. Matisee's Glosarry of Internet Terms http://www.matisse.net/files/glossary.html
53. MCI Web Sote Enterprise : Insight & Innovation : Cerf's Up http://global.mci.com/us/enterprise/insight/cerfs_up/
54. Microsoft Web Site http://www.microsoft.com

55. MIT www.mit.gov.in
56. Multimedia Search Engines-SearchTools Report http://www.searchtools.com/info/multimedia-search.html
57. NCST Web Site http://www.ncst.in
58. On the Net http://www.sla.org/pubs/serial/io/1997/feb97/net.html
59. Search SPIE Papers- Publications- SPIE WEB http://spie.org/scripts/abstract.pl?bibcode=1996SPIE%2e2670%2e%2e%2e88T&page=1&qs=spie
60. Sun Web site http://www.sun.com/products
61. Tech Review UpStream: Video Searching http://www.techreview.com/articles/upstream0701.asp
62. UNESCO www.unesco.org/webworld/participer/guidelines/index.htm
63. University of Delaware Library http://www.lib.udel.edu/
64. Virtual Library LibrarySpot http://www.libraryspot.com/
65. WhatIs http://www.whatis.com
66. IIT Bombay Web site www.iitb.ac.in
67. W3 Web site www.w3.org